Yesterday's Voices for Today's World

Yesterday's Voices for Today's World

Fred M. Wood

BROADMAN PRESS
Nashville, Tennessee

© Copyright 1967 • BROADMAN PRESS
All rights reserved

422–504

DEWEY DECIMAL CLASSIFICATION NUMBER: 224
Library of Congress Catalog Card Number: 67–17431
Printed in the United States of America
16. AL 67 K.S.P.

Affectionately Dedicated to
Dr. Clyde C. Francisco
who guided the author
in his early years of study
and continues to be a help
and inspiration

Preface

❦
❦

       I have closely followed **Fred Wood's** career since he left the Southern Baptist Theological Seminary. He was graduated with the seminary's highest degree, demonstrating unusual ability and unflagging energy. His pastorate at Eudora Baptist Church in Memphis, Tennessee, has been characterized by unusually significant progress. This outward success is rooted in a Bible-centered expository pulpit ministry that keeps the congregation in the mainstream of Christian tradition.

  Dr. Wood has been able to continue serious study despite the demanding responsibility of a city pastorate. This has strengthened his ministry and has helped his understanding of the relevancy of the Bible to life in today's world. This book on the prophets is a remarkable combination of scholarship, insight, and practical application. The reader will find himself strangely warmed and convincingly challenged.

Clyde T. Francisco

Contents

Contents

Acknowledgments

♣

Although I have received assistance from many persons in the preparation of this book, I am indebted to one man more than any other. Dr. Clyde Francisco, John R. Sampey professor of Old Testament at Southern Baptist Theological Seminary, has had the greatest and most profound influence.

Dr. Francisco first introduced me to the historical-critical approach in the interpretation of the Old Testament. He guided me during those early days of plowing new ground, adjusting to new knowledge, and gaining new insights.

I am most fortunate, also, to have a family that is in complete sympathy with my work. Without their understanding and love this book would not have been completed. By relieving me of many home duties they have given me more time for study and writing.

My secretary, Mrs. A. E. Gibson, made a tremendous contribution to this book. She helped in typing and in proofreading, and has offered many valuable suggestions. I am deeply indebted to her.

Other friends have encouraged and assisted. I wish to thank each for every help and suggestion.

FRED M. WOOD

1

A Privileged People
(AMOS)

In Greek philosophy, history was believed to occur in cycles. By contrast, Hebrew philosophy held that history moved toward a divine goal. One can accept the Hebrew philosophy of history and yet believe that history does repeat itself as it moves toward the goal of a divine will.

For this reason, the words of the Hebrew prophets are among the most important to have been spoken by man. These men, who never doubted the ultimate purpose of God in history, spoke truth that is timeless and applicable to all generations. Their moral and ethical insights have never been surpassed. To them, life was contingent upon compatibility with God. Others, intoxicated with the here and now, saw life in short-term values, but the concern of the prophets was its moral end.

Although rejected by his own generation, the herdsman from Tekoa speaks timeless truth with unequaled urgency to every age. The nation's leaders were guilty of accepting material blessings as a sign of moral approval and felt no obligation either to God or their fellowman. Israel believed that the Lord was her unconditional ally, regardless of con-

13

duct or attitude. This is a most dangerously deceptive position for either a nation or an individual. It brought forth one of the strongest indictments to be found in all the Old Testament: "You only have I known of all the families of the earth: therefore I will punish you for all your iniquities" (Amos 3:2).

A Position of Privilege

No nation has been blessed more abundantly than ancient Israel. From the beginning of her history she had been the object of divine revelation and love. The Lord had sought through natural calamities and disasters to discipline his people and through divine guidance to lead them to repentance. His righteousness had been revealed in the conquest of the land, and his divine love through prophets who directed the people to himself.

God's choice of Israel is the great love story of the ages. He did not choose Assyria with its military might nor Egypt with its centuries of civilization and culture. He chose a wandering Aramaean and an enslaved people whom he rescued from captivity. Moses described the beginning of God's people in striking words: "He found him in a desert land, and in the waste howling wilderness; he led him about, he instructed him, he kept him as the apple of his eye" (Deut. 32:10). Of the great deliverance the psalmist says, "When Israel went out of Egypt . . . Judah was his sanctuary, and Israel his dominion. The sea saw it, and fled: Jordan was driven back. The mountains skipped like rams, and the little hills like lambs" (114:1–4).

No other nation had been the object of such tender affection and revelation as had Israel when God chose this nation to be his own peculiar people. His purpose was to make Israel a kingdom of priests and a holy nation. Theodore Laetsch says, "This unique distinction implied a special obligation of love and obedience, a greater responsibility, and the certainty of severest punishment if they despised this single honor." Neither before nor since has a nation been called to such a relationship nor been the recipient of such priceless privileges.

Some people are born to a place of privilege. Others are not. Dr. Reuben Youngdahl says that in the world today the mathematical odds would not favor birth in a place of privilege. A person would have one chance out of three to be born white, one out of twenty to be born in America. He would be twice as likely to be born in India as in America. He would be five times as likely to be born in China. If he were born in India, he would have one chance in four of surviving the first year and only a fifty-fifty chance of reaching seven years of age. In many places he would go home to a windowless, small, mud hut with a dirt floor. Yet personal inconvenience would be his least problem. He would live in a disease-infested environment. His children would be weakened and wasted before his eyes. Most important, there would be no motivating presence of Christ in his heart, no hope for eternity, no abundant life, for he would have no opportunity to enter a Christian church to hear the gospel.

However, Amos did not speak to an underprivileged people, but to a highly favored nation to whom had been committed the oracles of God, a nation chosen to be the instrument through which he would bless the world. To that nation he had given a revelation of himself that would grow in the processes of time until it burst full bloom into the fulness of the knowledge of God in Jesus Christ. Israel's position of privilege was attained solely through the grace of God. Dr.

Roy Honeycutt says, "Privilege is with purpose, however, and no nation or individual can afford to forget that the corollary of privilege is responsibility."

To be specially endowed with unique ability or to be lavishly blessed with material advantages is both a priceless possession and a source of potential woe. Pusey says, "The nearer God places anyone to His own light, the more malignant is the choice of darkness instead of light." The great ones of history interpret superior status as an opportunity for greater service, but little people accept it with pride, complacency, and boasting, as pardon for the past and security for the future. Jesus warned, "For unto whomsoever much is given, of him shall be much required" (Luke 12:48).

A Period of Prosperity

Few eras in Israel's history were characterized by greater economic security and personal luxury than the reigns of Uzziah and Jeroboam II. Uzziah reigned fifty-two years in Judah and Jereboam for forty-three years in Israel. Almost simultaneously each brought a period of unparalleled prosperity to his country.

The author of 1 and 2 Kings, who measured Israel's rulers almost entirely by their spiritual contribution to their country, says little about Jeroboam. His observation tells only a part of the story. "He restored the coast of Israel from the entering of Hamath unto the sea of the plain" (2 Kings 14:25). Other sources reveal that under Jeroboam's dynamic and aggressive leadership Israel regained national glory and prestige comparable to the days of David and Solomon. Fortunately Jeroboam reigned at a time when the surrounding nations were either weak or involved with internal problems. Syria's power had been broken by Assyria, and Jeroboam was able to restore the territory that Syria had taken from Israel. Assyria was not yet strong enough to threaten the independence of Israel. Thus, under Jeroboam the land was free from foreign control and enjoyed a prosperous and self-sufficient economic situation.

The book of Amos vividly reflects the prosperity in Israel. The nation enjoyed unprecedented expansion in trade. A large group of merchants developed, becoming a class to themselves. Raymond Calkins says, "Wealth increased and luxuries abounded. Israel enjoyed an economic boom. Materialism was the order of the day with all the social abuses that follow such a rapid development in wealth."

The simple herdsman from Tekoa found a striking contrast when he left the wilderness of poverty and danger and journeyed to the shrine at Bethel and the other places of popular worship. The palaces of that day were built of hewn stone (Amos 5:11). Some of them were paneled with ivory (3:15). As he saw the pretentious summer and winter residences, with their extravagant interior finish, he could not avoid seeing and hearing the drunken revelries of the people who had forgotten their Lord. He could not be blind to the mad extravagance of the people. He noted that they found satisfaction only in possessing the best of everything—the chief ointments (6:6), the most delicate meats (6:4), and the best music (6:5.) The worship places reflected the general prosperity of the day. The sanctuaries at Bethel were subsidized by the king. No longer was the worship spiritual and marked by ethical constraint. The worship place was thronged with those who brought abundant gifts and celebrated the feasts with all possible pomp and enjoyment.

Riding the crest of a booming economy, Israel was unaware of the reality which would face her shortly. Roy L. Smith in *The Future is Upon Us* says, "There is nothing more tragic in the life of a nation or an individual . . . than to assume we are on a joy ride when we are headed for an abyss." Israel was on the "joy ride" of a postwar prosperity. However, there were ominous signs on the horizon. The discerning eyes of Amos saw beneath the tinseled surface of his day the symptoms of rottenness and certain decay. Actually, judgment was coming soon—very soon! Assyria was reorganizing her military affairs and was about to move westward with a mighty military machine. And Israel, pampered by plenty, softened with ease, and decaying of idleness, would shortly pay the price for too much luxury and too little concern for spiritual values.

A Perversion of Principles

Israel's sin was not a lack of religion. As Amos journeyed through the hill country of Ephraim, he saw the people meticulously observing the external requirements of religion, the mechanics of religious duty. They zealously presented their daily sacrifices, brought their tithes on the three annual festivals, and fulfilled all ritualistic requirements of the Law.

What then was the problem? Amos charged that their religion of ritual was so perverted and degenerate that it was only a cloak to cover their iniquity and transgression. R. E. Wolfe in *Meet Amos and Hosea* describes the situation: "Worship is actually a cause of sin. The more the Israelites worship, the more crime they feel free to commit. They love this false religion because it saves them from the weightier demands of justice and ethical religion."

Although Israel's sins are mentioned in various places throughout the book of Amos, they are perhaps best summarized in verses 6 through 8 of chapter 3. They were: unparalleled perversion of justice—"they sold the righteous for silver, and the poor for a pair of shoes" (2:6); unbelievable oppression of the downtrodden—they "pant after the dust of the earth on the head of the poor" (2:7); a thoroughgoing attempt to discredit sincere worshipers—they "turn aside the way of the meek" (2:7); and flagrant immorality accompanied by unbridled self-indulgence in open defiance of religious requirements and with utter disregard or reverence for spiritual customs and institutions—"a man and his father go in to the same maiden, . . . they lay themselves down beside every altar upon garments taken in pledge; and in the house of their God they drink the wine of those who have been fined" (2:7-8, RSV).

Amos made it clear that the women shared in the guilt and, indeed, were the force that drove men to ungodly conduct. He pictured the "cows of Bashan" as they "oppress the poor . . . crush the needy . . . say to their husbands, Bring, that we may drink!" (4:1, RSV). In every historical situation the women of a country determine and reflect the moral condition of the land. The prophet may have had in mind especially the women as he spoke of those who "lie upon beds of ivory . . . stretch themselves upon their couches . . . eat lambs from the flock . . . sing idle songs . . . drink wine in bowls . . . anoint themselves with the finest oils, but are not grieved over the ruin of Joseph!" (6:4-6, RSV). Ease and luxury soon make one insensitive to the needs of others.

Amos condemned the greedy, money-mad merchants who resented the religious festivals that interfered with remaining open for business, and who could hardly wait for the sabbath to pass so normal sales activity could be resumed. "When will the new moon be gone, that we may sell corn? and the sabbath, that we may set forth wheat?" (8:5). Amos further censored their business of "making the ephah small, and the shekel great, and falsifying the balances by deceit" (8:5). In their greed they wrongly sold even the refuse of the wheat which was supposed to be left for the poor to glean.

There were no formal courts housed in imposing public buildings such as we have today. Property disagreements were settled by the city gate where streams of people passed. The prominent and respected men of the city served as judges. People were summoned as witnesses and jury. Even though this was a crude approach, the people through the years had taken pride in meting out justice. By the time of Amos, however, the situation had degenerated to a perversion of justice on every hand. In their greed, the judges favored anyone in a decision who offered a bribe, large or small. If one could do no better, a pair of sandals would assure the verdict. Wolfe says, "Usually the last stand of respectability in a declining nation is found in her judiciary. With the degeneration of Israel's legal machinery, the fate of the nation seemed certain." Pointing to the multitude of their transgressions and the greatness of their sins, Amos called them a people who "afflict the righteous . . . take a bribe . . . turn aside the needy in the gate" (5:12, RSV). Realizing the forcefulness of his words he warned, "He who is prudent will keep silent in such a time; for it is an evil time" (5:13, RSV). Someone, with tongue in cheek, has paraphrased Amos' words, "If I had good sense I'd keep quiet about the whole mess." But Amos could not keep quiet. He was God's messenger. "The lion has roared. . . . The Lord God has spoken; who can but prophesy?" (3:8, RSV).

A Proclamation of Punishment

The Lord had previously chastised his people, but they had failed to heed his warnings. He had sent "cleanness of teeth" and "want of bread" (4:6), isolated showers and droughts (4:7), blasting, mildew, palmer-worms, pestilences, and raids by the enemy (4:9–11). The result, however, was always the same. The constant refrain is, "Yet have ye not returned unto me, saith the Lord" (4:6–11).

Israel's end is now near. So sure is Amos that his words take the form of a dirge in the doleful qinah measure and speak of Israel as a virgin who is already fallen, never to rise again, with no one who cares enough to lift her up (5:1–2).

When judgment comes it will be *thorough.* Any who might remain are compared to "two legs, or a piece of an ear" rescued by a shepherd out of the mouth of a lion (3:12). The punishment will be *cruel.* The enemy will take the people with hooks and even fishhooks (4:2). The judgment will be *all-inclusive.* None shall escape the captivity. Flight will perish from the swift . . . the strong will not strengthen his force, neither shall the mighty deliver himself. The bowman will not stand, the rider of the horse shall not be safe. Even the most courageous of the mighty shall flee away naked (2:13–16).

According to Amos, the coming judgment was certain and imminent. The prophet spoke of the Lord as one who brings sudden destruction upon the strong (5:9). He warned the people that though they had built houses of hewn stones they would not remain in them. Indeed, some who had only recently planted vineyards would not enjoy the wine from the fruit (5:11).

The people of Amos' day had a comfortable doctrine which afforded them serenity and satisfaction. They called it the "day of the Lord"—a day of victory when God would bless his people and honor them before their enemies. But to Amos, the day was one when God would vindicate his righteousness, would reward those who were faithful to his commands, and punish those who had transgressed his moral requirements. Amos shouted, "Woe to you who desire the day of the Lord! Why would you have the day of the Lord? It is darkness, and not light; as if a man fled from a lion, and a bear met him; or went into the house and leaned with his hand against the wall, and a serpent bit him" (5:18–19, RSV). The prophet was saying that the popular concept of the people was false. God would vindicate his righteousness principles and those who were obedient to them. Only they were really the people of God—the true Israel.

As Amos proclaimed the coming judgment he called the king by name, "I will rise against the house of Jeroboam with the sword" (7:9). At this point, Amaziah, the priest of Bethel, sent word to the king that the land was not able to bear the words of Amos, then ordered Amos to go back to Judah and prophesy there. He sarcastically called Amos a "seer," and by his expression "eat bread there" put Amos in the class of the popular ecstatics who were interested primarily, if not exclusively, in fees and honorariums. He forbade Amos to preach any more at Bethel, the sanctuary of the king. It was a royal house. In the language of today, "This is where Jeroboam the king has his membership!"

At this point the true character of Amos is seen and more about him is revealed than anywhere else. He was no professional; "I was no prophet . . . but I was an herdman, and a gatherer of sycomore fruit: And the Lord took me as I followed the flock, and the Lord said unto me, Go, prophesy unto my people Israel" (7:14–15). Fearlessly, he then pronounced one of the fiercest devastations to be found in his book. Because Amaziah dared to suggest that Amos should "soft-pedal" his message against Israel, he will learn that Jehovah would not spare religious leaders who compromise and suggest that others do the same. "Thy wife shall be an harlot in the city . . . thy sons and thy daughters shall fall by the sword . . . and thou shalt die in a polluted land: and Israel shall go into captivity" (7:17).

Although Amos occasionally interjected a command such as, "Seek . . . me, and ye shall live" (5:4), his message was that judgment was certain. The nation had gone too far in sin. Israel was morally incapable of repentance. She had passed the point of no return. Religious leaders and political leaders alike enjoyed the prosperity too much. Even at that moment the Lord was raising up a nation which would afflict Israel from one end of the land to the other and would take it into captivity beyond Damascus (5:27; 6:14). The soul (or nation) that sins shall surely die.

A Promise of Perpetuity

In the last few verses of the book the tone of the message changes entirely. No longer does the prophet warn of imminent judgment. Suddenly he becomes a prophet of hope, promising the people that the nation will not be destroyed but will be restored. He promises hyperbolic fertility of the soil and crops. He speaks of the plowman overtaking the reaper and the mountains dropping sweet wine (9:13).

Whether the words came from Amos of Tekoa or are the work of a later editor is a problem in biblical criticism. Modern scholarship tends to assign it to a later writer who wished to soften the harshness of Amos and give a hope for the future. However, many reliable scholars of all eras, including the modern, believe the words to be genuine utterances of the prophet Amos.

The point of this epilogue is clear and the spiritual teaching is relevant. God's holiness demands that he punish sin. However, the captivity was not to bring doom but discipline. God's purpose in history would not be defeated. A remnant would survive the captivity and form the nucleus of the kingdom of God in the future. Since national Israel would not be usable in God's purposes, he will seek within Israel the spiritual kernel who would be his people. Through this dedicated nucleus, God's purpose would eventually come to fruition.

What a lesson for God's people in every generation! Elton Trueblood in *The Life We Prize*, says, "If we take seriously . . . the philosophy of responsibility, we must recognize the burden which comes in necessary association with privilege. . . . Great advantages, far from giving us easy minds, should give us very uneasy minds. If the philosophy of responsibility is true our burden is heavy."

The herdsman from Tekoa is not merely a quaint spokesman from another day. He speaks to every civilization, especially to people highly favored and greatly blessed. God will bring his purposes to fulfilment—with men if he may, without them if he must, but God will go on! True wisdom is to learn where God is going and go with him!

2

A Rebel Reformed
(JONAH)

Amazing in depth of insight and unsurpassed in simple beauty, the book of Jonah is a literary and spiritual masterpiece. Its one great message glows contagiously with the author's dream and purpose. Other lessons taught are by-products of the truth that God loves all people regardless of who or where they are. German scholar C. H. Cornill once testified that although he had read the book at least a hundred times, he could not speak of it without tears rising to his eyes and his pulse beating faster. He insisted that it was one of the deepest and grandest books ever written.

However, a tragedy concerning this marvelous book exists. It has become the center of a controversy between two schools of thought. One group says it must be historically factual or else it loses its spiritual value. Another, equally sincere, says that some of the greatest spiritual messages ever delivered to mankind were presented in parabolic form.

Let it be admitted that the school of literal interpretation has proved it *could* have happened! Large fish *have* been found which are fully capable of swallowing a man. An amusing anecdote tells of an educationally underprivileged preacher who saw such a fish in a museum. Every few minutes he loudly exclaimed, "Praise the Lord." After being warned several times to maintain silence, he apologetically explained to the custodian, "I'm sorry to disturb the others, but you see I'm a preacher. I've been preaching about Jonah for forty years, and I've never really believed it until now." Certainly Christians are not fair with the evidence nor consistent in their belief in the sovereignty and resourcefulness of God unless they agree that the story is historically possible. Phillips Brooks jokingly said that the story posed no insuperable problem, for after all Jonah was only one of the minor prophets.

The problem is, however, did the author mean for this story to be taken literally? When one group argues that Jesus spoke of Jonah as a historical character, the other replies that today literary allusions are made to personalities such as Macbeth or Hamlet, and the hearers know that these characters had no actual existence. One of the most logical statements concerning the matter has been made by Dean Farrar, "If it could be shown that Jesus intended by these words to stamp the story as literally true, every Christian would at once . . . accept it. But this is an assumption, and it is a bad form of uncharitableness to adopt the tone of those commentators who charge their opponents with setting aside the authority of Christ. Seeing that our Lord so largely adopted the method of moral allegory in his own parabolic teaching—seeing that it was part of his habit to embody truths in tales which were not literal facts, but were only told to fix deep spiritual lessons in the minds of the hearers—nothing is more possible than that he should have pointed to the deep symbolism of an Old Testament parable without at all intending to imply that the facts actually happened." [1]

Reasonable as it seems, this conclusion does not satisfy all interpreters. Many feel that the chief motive of those who deny a literal interpretation is to eliminate the supernatural elements in the book. On the other hand, a scholar like Dr. R. W. Dale of Birmingham, England, says, "I receive without a shadow of doubt many miraculous stories of actual facts, but this book, on the whole, looks to me unlike a story of actual facts."

However, to receive and apply the spiritual message of the story is more important than trying to solve the problem which has divided the scholars for centuries. Awed by the tremendous task of world missions, a young man once asked the Duke of Wellington whether or not Christians were really obligated to carry the gospel message to everyone. Wellington asked, "What are the marching orders of your Commander?" When the young man quoted the Great Commission, Wellington replied, "You have no choice. A soldier always obeys his commander." The militant message of the gospel throbs in each sentence with the story of the prophet who learned the hard way that God's love extends to all people. This voice still speaks across the centuries saying that the missionary message is no mere elective in Christianity's curriculum.

Disobedience

The book of Jonah is more than the story of a man. It is a picture of a nation's attitude. Alexander Maclaren says, "Israel was set, not as a dark lantern, but as the great lampstand in the Temple court proclaimed to ray out light to all the world." Jonah's mission was a symbol of Israel's mission to be a messenger to all nations. His refusal to go to Nineveh represented the national feelings which he shared.

Jonah was a patriotic and popular preacher when the call came to go to Nineveh. He shared the zeal of every loyal Israelite for his country. According to the historical writer, he spoke optimistically and encouragingly concerning the conquest of Jeroboam and the extension of Israel's border. It must have been a blow to Jonah's pride and a threat to his image to be told to go tell Nineveh that God had a place for them in his program.

Jonah's refusal to go to Nineveh was not because of the hazards involved nor because he felt the mission to be a hopeless one. He feared that he would be successful. Nineveh would repent. God would forgive them. They would share with Israel in God's favor. The prophet's reputation would then suffer. Jonah's spirit was similar to that of the prodigal son's elder brother.

The exact manner in which the "word of the Lord came to Jonah" is not clear. Circumstances vary with individuals. Many have been moved by the "still small voice" which spoke silently and convincingly of God's will. As such persons ponder experiences and issues of moral and ethical significance, they become increasingly aware of God's will for their life. James H. Kennedy in *Studies in the Book of Jonah* says, "While reflecting on . . . some spiritual verity spoken by a humble and impassioned witness to truth, they have had impressions progressively to deepen into value judgments and ultimately to crystallize into sure convictions on life's meaning and purpose and task."

Underlying all concepts of sin is one great truth. Sin is rebellion against the will of God. It is the disobedience of a will opposed to God's plan and purpose for that life. God wanted Jonah to go to Nineveh. Jonah did not want to go. It was that simple. Other factors may have been present, but the

basic one was that Jonah's wish was pitted against God's
will.

One is on the road to spiritual maturity when he has
learned to obey. Shallow minds resent obedience to a superior,
but Aeschylus calls obedience "the mother of success" and
George Macdonald speaks of it as "the key to every door."
In military circles, the best commander is the one who has
first learned to obey. John Milton wrote

> Who best
> Can suffer, best can do; best reign, who first
> Well hath obeyed.

In this day when any form of authority seems to be resented,
we need to understand that through obedience one learns to
command. A great Christian of another generation said, "I
find doing the will of God leaves me no time for disputing
about his plans."

Rebellion against God's will usually causes one to take the
opposite direction. It was true with Jonah. Running from God,
he decided to go as far to the west as God wanted him to go
to the east. Most scholars agree that the Tarshish to which
Jonah booked passage was not Tarsus of Asia Minor but a
town in Spain which was a commercial outpost. Rather than
go to a great metropolitan center in the midst of the known
world, Jonah would rather lose himself at the edge of the
earth's civilization.

Three times in the first ten verses the record is that Jonah
sought to escape from "the presence of the Lord." Some
scholars insist that Jonah shared the common opinion of the
pagans that each God was a tribal god and his influence was
limited to his own territory. This is not probable, however,

for Jonah would not have felt the necessity to go such an extreme distance had this been his concept of God. Jonah was simply trying to get away from a distasteful assignment, and he thought that geographical distance would lend spiritual immunity. Not all who rebel against God's will are able to put miles between themselves and their native soil. There are other ways of going in an opposite direction. Indifference to the Lord's work or immoral indulgences may be the Tarshish of modern Jonahs who are running from God's will.

Deliverance

Clovis Chappell says, "God never allows us to wreck ourselves by our foolish rebellion without doing his infinite best to save us." Shakespeare utters this same truth a bit differently, "There's a divinity that shapes our way, rough hew it as we will." The sea of the rebel's voyage is never smooth; it is rough with storms. Only in God's will is the calm of peace to be found.

The story of Jonah's voyage is well known. The Scriptures make it clear that God sent the storm. As in the New Testament, so in the story of Jonah, "The winds and the sea obeyed him." The waves tossed the boat to and fro. Theodore Laetsch pictures the ship as "one moment it hung perilously trembling on the crest of a large wave, only to be hurled into the yawning abyss until it was covered with water."

During this convulsion of natural forces Jonah had retreated into some obscure corner wishing to remain unnoticed. While the others battled the raging elements, he slept soundly. The sixty-mile journey from Gath-hepher to Joppa had exhausted him physically. The mental and spiritual agony through which he had gone left him emotionally drained. In desperation, the sailors were crying to their various gods. Jonah, who knew the true God, was at perfect ease with no burden for anyone's welfare or safety. For the moment, he was at peace with the world, believing, as many like-minded persons do today, he had removed himself from the jurisdiction of God.

The suddennness and violence of the storm with its whirlwind force convinced the shipmaster this was no ordinary tempest. He sought an explanation and investigated every possibility. When other prayers failed, he invaded Jonah's privacy and demanded that he pray to his God. Whether Jonah uttered a petitionary word is not clear, but finally the decision was made to cast lots to determine "for whose cause this evil has come." When the lot fell upon Jonah he admitted guilt. There is a nobility among the mariners who first refused to cast Jonah overboard, even after he had confessed his rebellion against the Lord. They made every effort to bring the boat back to land without following Jonah's suggestion that he should be cast into the sea. Only as a last resort did they throw Jonah overboard. They finally decided their deliverance depended upon it. A study of the words "God" and "Yahweh" (translated "Lord" in the KJV) in the passage reveal a significant fact. At the close of the account the sailors are praying to Jonah's God, offering sacrifices, and making vows unto him. Had this experience made them believers in the true God?

It is difficult to know Jonah's thoughts in that fleeting moment as he disappeared beneath the waves. The poem in chapter 2 records his thanksgiving to God for deliverance. It is not the poem of a man on dry land, grateful to God for deliverance from the whale. It is a prayer of Jonah while still in the fish's belly. The deliverance for which Jonah sang praises was from a watery grave which he called "the belly of Sheol."

Actually, the big fish was not his punishment but his salvation. Otherwise he would have drowned.

Did Jonah repent of his disobedience while still in the water, or did it take a three-day confinement to break his stubborn spirit? Two statements in his prayer of praise indicate a mellowing of his defiant attitude while still in the sea. He said, "All thy billows and thy waves passed over me. . . . I said, I am cast out of they sight; yet I will look again toward thy holy temple" (2:3-4). Later in the poem he declared, "When my soul fainted within me I remembered the Lord: and my prayer came in unto thee" (2:7). Perhaps even before he was rescued by the fish he had resolved to re-establish fellowship with God if only he could be saved from what looked to be certain death.

Regardless of when the transformation came, it did come. It may be that the poem of praise was the deciding factor that led God to give Jonah a second chance. The text can be so interpreted. A wise man learns he cannot hold out against God. An even wiser man yields to God's plan early in his life and has no "years in sinning wasted" which he would fain recall and live again.

While in college the writer read two biographies the same week. One was of Jerry McAuley, the other of John A. Broadus. It took the former many years of rebelling and repenting in an "on again—off again" kind of life before he surrendered completely to God's will. Though his sincerity is unquestioned, his contribution was limited. John Broadus, however, found God's purpose early and began immediately to fulfil it. Few men have equaled the career of this man whom God kept on double duty as preacher and teacher for more than half a century. Although a man can receive salvation from Christ after a wasted life or make full commitment of talents after years of rebellion, the wasted years can never quite be restored.

Dedication

Dr. Kyle M. Yates calls chapter 3 "Jonah running with God" in contrast to the first two chapters—"Jonah running from God" and "Jonah running to God." Whatever reluctance Jonah may have had to obey God is now gone. When the word of the Lord came the second time, Jonah arose and went unto Nineveh.

Essentially, a godly life is obedience to the revealed will of God. This is not a life of blind performance to the externals of a mechanical legalism. But when the path of duty to God's will is clear, one has no alternative. John Wesley once said, "To find God's will is man's greatest discovery, to do God's will is man's greatest achievement."

Jonah had but one message as he entered a third of the way into Nineveh. Literally, the Hebrew says, "Forty days and Nineveh—overthrown." The warning was not accompanied by any warmhearted invitation to repentance. It was a cold statement of fact. The Hebrew verb implies that Jonah could see the city being destroyed before his eyes. Nineveh's doom was certain.

In spite of the preacher's stern, compassionless message, the people believed the message. The record tells of an amazing repentance. The people put on sackcloth. They proclaimed a fast. When news reached the king, he also put on sackcloth and covered himself with ashes. His decree was quite comprehensive: "Let neither man nor beast, herd nor flock, taste anything; let them not feed, or drink water, but let man and beast be covered with sackcloth, and let them cry mightily to God; yea, let everyone turn from his evil way and from the violence which is in his hands. Who knows, God may yet repent and turn from his fierce anger, so that we perish not?" (3:7-9, RSV).

Those who insist that this account is not to be interpreted literally point out there is no place in the framework of Assyrian national life to fit this wholesale repentance into a historical context. This is not exactly accurate. The reigns of several kings preceding Tiglath-Pileser's rise to power in 745 B.C. provide the possibility of such a setting. These weak kings were lackadaisical about morals and religion. Quite possibly, there could have been a day of national mourning when this Hebrew prophet warned of a coming crisis. Later, God sent Nahum to warn the people again when they returned to their iniquities. Profound scholarship does not build a dogmatic case on what is not known. Jonah actually lived (cf. 2 Kings 14:25). Is a parabolic interpretation fair to this historical character?

God never closes his ear to the cry of genuine repentance. Jonah had learned some unforgettable lessons during his stern chastisement. This discipline of distress was almost equal to returning from the dead. If ever a man preached with urgency, it was this Hebrew prophet with whom God had dealt so convincingly.

In all generations, great preaching by dedicated men has made the difference in a nation's destiny. If the pulpit remains silent on moral and spiritual issues, injustice will sweep the land. No people ever degenerated into sin and iniquity but that the men in the pulpits first became weak and indifferent. "Let the pulpit decay and the cause of Christ is lost. Nothing can take the place of preaching. There is no power under heaven equal to the power of a God-inspired pulpit . . . the exposition of God's Word by a man whose lips have been touched by a coal from off God's altar." The sure way to hopelessly handicap God's work is for preachers to forget to preach truth forcefully. The central truth of the book of Jonah is its missionary outreach, but there is certainly a tribute to great preaching by a dedicated man with a sense of urgency because of a divine call.

Disappointment

The book Jonah ends where it began—with the prophet in rebellion to the will of God. The background is that of Jonah's failure to understand how God could love everyone, regardless of who or where he is. This particular attitude however, was but the symptom of a deeper deficiency and emotional need in Jonah's life.

In stressing the missionary message of the story a more fundamental fact about the prophet may be missed. Jonah's real problem was disappointment and belligerence because God would not conform to his concept of God. In this attitude, Jonah was a symbol of the entire nation.

This was Israel's problem throughout her history. God demanded holiness in character and worship. Israel sought to win God's favor by performing meticulously the externals of ritual requirements as a substitute for his higher demands. Israel thought that Jehovah was her unconditional ally regardless of moral and ethical standards. But God said Israel would be his own possession "if ye will obey my voice indeed, and keep my covenant" (Ex. 19:5). Israel interpreted the day of the Lord as meaning a time in which all the enemies of Israel would be exterminated, but God meant it to be a time when his righteousness would be vindicated and his principles victorious. The people thought that being a part of national Israel was the greatest security and the surest way to God's favor. Throughout Old Testament history, God tried to show the people the truth Peter finally perceived, "In every nation any one who fears him and does what is right is acceptable to him" (Acts 10:35, RSV).

In every generation there are some good people who, like Jonah, fail to see God's larger programs and to understand that leaders must share his compassion for all mankind. Even after his experience at Nineveh, Jonah still was emotionally incapable of seeing the world through the eyes of God.

Jonah's pride was a chief problem. He had warned the people of coming judgment; but when the crisis was averted, he interpreted God's mercy to the repentant people as a repudiation of his message and an affront to him personally. God's object lesson with the gourd was unusual indeed, but the prophet could not have missed the point. Jonah's pride had turned his scale of values topsy-turvy. He had become far more concerned for his own physical comfort than for the spiritual condition of people.

Jonah's experience is relevant today. James H. Kennedy says that the supreme issue for our modern world is "gourds or souls?" He asks, "What resources are to have priority, the moral and spiritual, or the economic and material? Are we further to succumb to a things-centered life, to a materialistic philosophy whose only passion is at the physical level? This is the choice of crucial importance to our own great nation." Roger Babson puts it equally urgent, "In the last analysis our national future depends upon our national character, that is, whether we are spiritually or materially minded."

The real test of a person's love for people is whether he loves individuals and is willing to forego personal convenience in order to share God's message with them. While helping a friend in an evangelistic revival in a small rural town, a minister visited in a third minister's home one afternoon. The midsummer temperature outside was in the high nineties. Inside the home an air-conditioner made the room pleasantly cool. The two preachers discussed some recent books on contemporary theology. Especially were they interested in evaluating modern theories on "the kingdom of God." Suddenly, remembering visits which needed to be made in homes in spiritual need, the visiting minister arose. "I must go," he said, then added with a smile, "It's a lot easier and far more comfortable to sit here and talk about concepts of the kingdom than to go out and seek people for the King and the kingdom. But I know which is the more important."

The book of Jonah has greater value than being the source of forensic debate as to its literary nature and interpretation. It is God's voice to all generations—his urgent voice saying,

> Red and yellow, black and white,
> They are precious in His sight.

"Go ye into all the world, and preach the gospel to every creature" (Mark 16:15).

> World need, world need, world need,
> We thank thee dear God for the chance of it,
> And the reach and the risk and romance of it,
> The high hope of it, the strong cope of it,
> And the way and the sway and the stay
> That comes now for the task for today.[2]

Notes

1. F. W. Farrar, *The Minor Prophets* (New York: Anson D. R. Randolph and Company), p. 234.

2. From a poem entitled "World Need" by E. P. Aldredge. Used by permission of the Sunday School Board of the Southern Baptist Convention.

3

Haughty Capital—Haunted Ruins
(NAHUM)

Nineveh's repentance at the preaching of Jonah was short-lived. By the middle of the seventh century B.C. Assyria was once more a cesspool of iniquity, a bloody city full of lies and rape. By this time the people must have become emotionally incapable of repentance, for Nahum assumed destruction as certain and imminent.

One great theme pervades this book. The haughty capital of the empire must be destroyed. This proud pagan citadel's doom is sealed. He who controls the forces of nature will not allow the guilty to remain unpunished. Although the mills of the Gods grind slowly, they grind exceedingly small.

The date of Nahum's prophecy can be fixed between two dates not far apart. He foretells Nineveh's destruction. Thus, he preached before 012 B.C., the date of the fall of Nineveh. He reminded the people that they were no better than the people of No-Amon (Thebes) who were carried away into captivity (3:8) in 668 B.C. So, he preached sometime between these two dates.

Some scholars have called Nahum's prophecy the least worthy of all Old Testament books in the canon. Some have denied that it deserves any place in the holy Scriptures. Julius Bewer calls him "the least attractive of the prophets" and maintains that in the history of religion he holds an inferior place. George Adam Smith calls him a "worse prophet than Zephaniah, with less conscience and insight." C. H. Cornill, a German scholar, says, "In a religious sense . . . the contents of the book are not important." Robert Pfeiffer speaks of Nahum as containing "nothing specifically religious" while Cadman insists, "no right-minded person" can approve of Nahum's contentions and attitudes. Karl Marti goes so far as to brand him, with his intense nationalism, as one of the false prophets against whom Jeremiah labored so vehemently.

Such accusations are grossly unfair. The presuppositions upon which they are based are not valid. One is not self-righteous because he condemns sin, nor is he a blind bigot because he is loyal to his nation and to the revelation he possesses of God.

One can be righteously indignant at unreasonable, unashamed, and unceasing defiance of God's moral law. One is justified in crying out against perversion of justice and morality. There are times when men rejoice in God's vengeance, not out of delight in suffering, but because it strengthens and assures those who seek to live in accordance with God's holiness. Nahum has an important place in history and prophecy.

Although the book's theme is the certainty of Nineveh's destruction, another great truth is woven in and out the fabric of the prophet's message. Jehovah is God. He rules in righteousness. God, not man, is supreme. J. Wallace Hamilton says that this fact was written into man's life without his vote. It existed before he arrived on the scene and will continue after his exit. God's throne is unshakable. Hamilton asks with tongue in cheek, "Do you suppose God will resign his sovereignty until the sociologists make up their minds about him?"

> It's the river that's lost if it misses the sea;
> If the sea miss the river, what matter?
> The sea is the sea forever.[1]

What kind of God is the Lord? Is he relevant to modern needs? Does he deserve a place in contemporary society? This book aids the quest for reality in understanding deity. Nahum's prophecy gives pertinent facts about the God and Father of the Lord, Jesus Christ.

Slow to Anger

The history of God's relation with Nineveh testifies to his patience in dealing with sin and sinners. The Old Testament shows repeatedly that God never acts in judgment without sending many warnings. Wolfendale says, "He never smites without first threatening. He is very slow to threaten. When God threatens, how slow He is to sentence the criminal! And when the sentence is signed and sealed, how slow to carry it out!"

God is slow to anger because he restrains himself in love. Possessing all resources within his own character, he sees the end from the beginning. The person who knows all can forgive all; the one who has abundant internal resources can remain calm under the most difficult circumstances. Undergirding all of this is God's love and reluctance to act, waiting to the last moment for the guilty one to repent and change his way of life.

Nineveh had been given every opportunity to amend her

ways. Her history, dating back at least to the time of Hammurabi (*ca.* 2200 B.C.), was, for centuries, of little significance, according to inscriptions concerning it. The early part of the ninth century saw Nineveh develop military strength and conquest, but a retrogression occured shortly afterwards which lasted about a century. With the coming of Tiglath-pileser to the throne in 745 B.C., the mighty military machine was formed. Shalmaneser (727–722 B.C.), Sargon (722–705 B.C.) and Sennacherib (705–681 B.C.) completed the "big four" or "murderer's row" which eliminated the Northern Kingdom and dominated the Southern Kingdom until the "angel of the Lord smote 185,000 Assyrian warriors" and Sennacherib hobbled back to Nineveh to die by the hand of his sons.

The three kings who followed were not as administratively strong as the preceding four, but cruelty and bloodshed continued. The moral situation within the country not only did not improve, it became increasingly worse. The Lord's eyes remained on Nineveh as she approached the day of wrath and the revelation of God's righteous judgment.

The Lord is slow to anger and his judgments are never capricious or unfair. He does not act with the whim of a cruel tyrant, nor does his rage flare up unpredictably and unreasonably with the fury of one who has not learned to control his temper. He is no hothead striking out and letting his blows fall without purpose or pattern. He gives the sinner every opportunity to fit into the overarching objective for his life. It is not his will that any should perish. God's reluctance to act punitively is a part of his goodness which leads to repentance.

To say God is "slow to anger" is another way of saying he is patient. Patience has more than one meaning. Words are like stars. One, shining in the sky, appears to be a solitary star, but a telescope reveals that two blazing lights have united to produce one great beam. Many small words seem like a "single star" until they are examined closely. Then, the word communicates a twofold message. A patient person can mean one who endures tribulation without complaint. But the word means more. It means also to wait calmly for a desired purpose to be achieved. This meaning of the word reveals the true nature of patience as related to God. He has a purpose. He wants all mankind to share in it. As long as any evidence exists that an individual or a nation will fit into his plan, God will go the third, even the fourth, mile. He will not blaze up in anger and consume man. Although people are irreverent, ungrateful, and rebellious, refusing to do God's will and persisting in doing the things that satisfy their vanity, he stands by waiting for men to come to their senses. "He will not strike us down. He will give us another day and still another, saying, 'Perhaps tomorrow the sin will be repented of and the prodigal will come home.'"

Unchangeable in Purpose

Although God is loving and longsuffering, let no one presume upon his kindness or compassion. There is a point of no return. Nineveh had reached it and had exhausted the divine patience. History reveals the devastating results. This city was to experience the same barbarous cruelties she had inflicted upon her neighbors in that ancient world. Nahum described what God must do in order to vindicate his sovereign righteousness. He must demonstrate to all the world that no one can defy his moral law without being broken asunder upon the rocks of rebellion.

After decreeing the certainty of Nineveh's doom, Nahum so

vividly describes the event that he seems to be an eyewitness. The definiteness of the description reveals the prophet's certainty that the event would happen and that it would happen soon. The majestic and moving style of the prophet carries the reader along on the crest of his inspired enthusiasm and poetic inspiration. The cruelties and savagery of the siege are described so vividly and with such a graphic attention to detail that the reader feels he is actually viewing the horrors and destruction.

Three stages in Nineveh's fall are described. First, fighting begins in the outskirts of the city. Second, the walls which encircled the city and afforded it protection from invasion are attacked. Third, the city is captured and despoiled. The attitude of the outside world toward Nineveh's fate is revealed in the last verse of the book, "All who hear the news of you clap their hands over you. For upon whom has not come your unceasing evil?" (3:19, RSV).

What is the purpose of such descriptions? What spiritual profit is there in outbursts of this kind? What warrants these words a place in the Holy Scriptures? The Lord is working his purpose in the world. Assyria was used to discipline Israel (the Northern Kingdom). Later, Babylon was used to chastise Judah (the Southern Kingdom). But when these divine instruments became filled with pride and self-importance, they forfeited their place of usefulness. Still later, Persia was used by God to make possible the return of the Jews to their homeland, but the time came when it was necessary for Persia to be removed. History reveals that God's purpose in the affairs of men is of prime importance. "The nations are as a drop of a bucket, and are counted as the small dust of the balance" (Isa. 40:15). A man or nation has value and stability only as he is related to the divine purpose. The grass withers and the flower fades, but the one who is in harmony with the divine plan shall abide forever.

A Stronghold in Trouble

While Israel was camped at Sinai, God made the people an encouraging promise; "If thou shalt . . . do all that I speak; then I will be an enemy unto thine enemies, and an adversary unto thine adversaries" (Ex. 23:22). Shortly before they entered the Promised Land, God gave them a further word of assurance: "If thou shalt hearken diligently unto the voice of the Lord thy God . . . The Lord shall cause thine enemies that rise up against thee to be smitten before thy face: they shall come out against thee one way, and flee before thee seven ways" (Deut. 28:1-7). Throughout the Old Testament this truth of God's involvement and identification with his people is repeated.

The message of Nahum is more than a tirade against Assyrian tyranny and heartless bloodshed. To see only this is to miss the greatest passages of the book. The prophet assured Judah that God was interested in her welfare and had an ear open to her need. Nahum affirmed the concern of God for his people as he declared, "The Lord is good, a strong hold in the day of trouble; and he knoweth them that trust in him" (1:7). After having spoken of the one who went forth out of Nineveh (probably referring to Sennacherib) to devise wickedness against Jehovah (v. 11), Nahum promised Judah that such men of worthlessness shall never pass through their land again but shall be cut off (v. 15). Because God cares for his people, he will pursue their enemies into darkness (v. 8).

These words were not promises of automatic safety to Judah regardless of the people's attitude toward sin. The conditional element is always present in God's promises, whether directly stated or not. The Lord is never the unconditional ally of a disobedient people. Nineveh however, had taken unfair advantage of Judah and had humbled her mercilessly. Such conduct must be punished by a righteous God. Judah was exhorted to celebrate the coming of the bearer of good tidings by keeping their solemn feasts and performing their vows (v. 15). The Lord would vindicate both himself and his people. He would restore the excellency of Jacob. Those who had emptied others would be emptied.

Nineveh had defied every precept of morality and decency. She had been full of witchcraft and harlotry. God, therefore, would strip her naked before the nations and show her to be a vile thing (3:5-6). Judah had not been perfect, but she was God's own peculiar possession. Judah had a unique relation to the Lord. She must be chastised for her delinquency, but she would not be cut off. God had a purpose for her. Judah's security was in doing the will of God and trusting him completely.

Relevant to Our Day

Does this book which Dean Farrar calls "less directly spiritual than the prophecies of Hosea, Isaiah and Micah" have any message for contemporary life? Many believe that it has a significant word which is needed by all who are caught up in the web of hatred, oppression, and iniquity which is choking the country.

Many scholars speak of the lyric beauty and picturesque vividness of the Hebrew poetry in this book. It contains more, however, than the aesthetic appeal of a rhythmic movement and the choice vocabulary of a literary masterpiece.

Nahum focuses on the moral government of God. In our day

when absolutes are questioned and the basis of morality is a controversial subject, it is reassuring to read the words of one who boldly declared the sovereignty and holiness of God. Nahum denounced specific sins. He was not fearful lest someone would label him a bigot, a legalist, or a prude. A recent writer criticised Billy Graham for preaching against sin, saying that "too much talk about sin is apt to stir up several varieties of guilt feelings with lamentable Freudian results." It is doubtful that such criticism by the freethinkers of his day would have bothered Nahum any more than this contemporary evaluation disturbed Billy Graham. Contemporary society, with its weakened moral integrity and spiritual anarchy, hypnotized by the delusion that it can compromise without judgment, *needs* a "guilt feeling." Speaking in biblical language, many thoughtful people would say that contemporary society needs to be convicted by the Holy Spirit of the iniquity of its transgression until it cries out to a holy God, "I have sinned against heaven and in thy sight."

Nahum proclaimed that there were no favorites with God. Nineveh was no better than Thebes who had built fortresses and imagined that the natural protection by the sea would make her invulnerable to the enemy. Yet she was carried away into captivity; her young children were dashed into pieces. They cast lots for her honorable men, and her great men were bound with chains (3:10). Nineveh also would fall because she had defied God's moral law. Her "strong holds shall be like fig trees with the firstripe figs: if they be shaken, they shall even fall into the mouth of the eater" (v. 12). No nation, or individual, is immune to the moral law of sin and retribution.

Shining through the fierceness of Nahum's declarations, however, is a final truth. God approves and protects those who take refuge in him. Although the door of opportunity may close upon a nation of people because of repeated refusal to hear and heed God's call, individuals may be saved. If enough individuals return to God and take seriously his claims, even a nation decaying morally can be redeemed. This is the only sure cure for a sick society and the only hope of a declining nation.

NOTES

1. Author unknown. Quoted by J. Wallace Hamilton, *Who Goes There?* (Westwood, N. J.: Fleming H. Revell Co., 1958).

4

Pure Religion Proclaimed
(MICAH)

About the same time that the peerless Isaiah
was nearing the middle of his ministry in the religious
capital of Jerusalem, an unsophisticated rustic began his
preaching in the region of Moresheth-gath, a small village
about twenty-five miles southwest of the great city. Both men
were prophets of God, possessed of individual, supplementary
characteristics which contributed to the religious life of Judah
and to the eternal purposes of God. Christendom would be
poorer without the contributions of both, for all generations
need the truths which each in his own way pronounced.

Isaiah was born an aristocrat. Tradition maintains that royal
blood flowed through his veins. Micah had no such heritage.
He was a man of lowly origin, a son of the soil, a thoroughgoing "grass rooter." Isaiah was the friend and confidante of
royalty; Micah associated with the lowly and never lost the
common touch. To Isaiah, God's purposes were aligned in-
separably with Jersualem. Micah had about the same regard
for Jerusalem as a Southern plantation owner has for New
York City. Isaiah was concerned with national and international politics. Micah was burdened for moral and ethical

righteousness which he regarded as a cosmic demand. God had a place for each of these men!

Although Micah lived in days of political significance, the prophet seemed entirely disinterested in the great international movements. His ministry was begun only a few years before the Northern Kingdom fell to Assyria. This removed the buffer state which protected Judah from the foreign invader. In spite of this alarming situation, virtually no word concerning the potential peril of the Assyrian menace appears in the book of Micah.

Why was Micah seemingly so detached from contemporary events? One answer is that the prophet was a countryman. Raymond Calkins maintains that his book reveals how dear the countryside was to him. The region in which Micah lived was one of small villages in the foothills of Judah, remote from the large towns and cities and the political activities that centered in Jerusalem.

To say that Micah was disassociated from the political events of the day does not mean that he was unaware of Judah's immoral conduct and the destiny to which it was leading the nation. Indeed, this was the heart of his message. Calkins says, "No man ever loved his native soil more than Micah. Yet no one ever uttered a sterner or more uncompromising message of merited retribution for flagrant sins than he." Micah saw the oppression of the poor and the injustices borne by the people. He says little concerning sensuality and sexual immorality. He is concerned largely with social sins—cruelty, oppressions, and man's inhumanity to man. His messages reveal a heart in agony because of oppression of his neighbors. To Micah, the cause of all evil was the love of the material, and wickedness was centered in the great teeming cities. Here dwelt the cruel, overbearing sophisticates who made the poor the victims of their greed. John R. Sampey said, "Micah snorted every time he saw a city." Micah was a strong personality with an independent spirit, an individualist who reflected the influence of his environment.

The book of Micah contains three distinct divisions, each emphasizing separate truths, yet blending into a comprehensive monogram concerning the moral and ethical needs of Judah. The message of Micah may best be presented by three questions: (1) What is the root and result of sin? (chaps. 1–3); (2) What is God's purpose in history? (chaps. 4–5); (3) What does God really want from man? (chaps. 6–8).

Root and Result of Sin (1–3)

Without any explanation of the nature of the people's transgressions, Micah immediately declares God's decree against the land and his determination to bring judgment upon it. Although his words may be classified as both anthropomorphic and apocalyptic, they have a ring of reality: "The Lord cometh forth out of his place, and will come down, and tread upon the high places of the earth. . . . the mountains shall be molten under him, and the valleys shall be cleft, as wax before the fire, and as the waters that are poured down a steep place" (1:3–4). This is the witness of the Lord against a sinful land. Micah calls upon all the people to hearken to God's message.

What made such judgment a necessity? Micah plainly states that the sin and degeneracy of the land is due to the concentration of wickedness and greed in the cities: "What is the transgression of Jacob? is it not Samaria? and what are the high places of Judah? are they not Jerusalem?" (1:5). To Micah, the great cities of the land embodied the corruption infecting the nation. The greed, idleness, and love of luxury present in the cities were the symbol of all that was base and wicked. The sin of the land was its cities!

Cities are not altogether bad. God has used them for great purposes and to begin great movements. Thoughtful men in every age have realized that large cities make little contribution to the spiritual life of a nation. Rousseau called cities "the sink of the human race" and Dean Inge said in his day, "The modern town dweller has no God and no devil; he lives without awe, without admiration, without fear." Even Thomas Jefferson declared, "The mob of great cities add just so much to the support of pure government as sores do to the strength of the human body." Micah has had his supporters in all generations!

False prophets were another cause of the land's depravity. These men pretended to be spokesmen for God, but were actually leaders in causing the people to sin. How did they do it? They were men who would "bite with their teeth" (3:5). This means that their chief concern in life was to fill their stomachs with food and wine. They willingly gave approval to those who put food in their mouths, but had only rebuke for those who contributed nothing to their well-being. These prophets were indifferent to moral truth and content to wink at the sensuality of the people in order to remain acceptable and rank high in their estimation.

Micah pictures the false prophet preaching to the people what they want to hear: "If a man should go about and utter wind and lies, saying, 'I will preach to you of wine and strong drink,' he would be the preacher for this people!" (2:11, RSV). Rolland Emerson Wolfe suggests that the phrase should be translated "for wine and strong," to indicate that if the people would supply the drink he desired, he would preach what they wanted to hear. However, other translators are more likely correct in the interpretation that the prophet will sanction any vice in which the people engage, if the people will receive him with open arms, retain him as their religious leader, and keep him on the payroll. Whichever interpretation is correct, the result is the same. The pew ruled the pulpit, and the chief criterion in selecting a preacher was that he deliver a message pleasing to the people rather than the bitter truth of certain punishment for sin.

Another area of Judah's iniquity was described by Micah. The land was filled with violence and greed. The prophet vividly portrayed the conduct of the heartless monopolists who lay awake at night planning how to exploit the poor of the land and seize all their earthly possessions. Any kind of evil is offensive, but when it is deliberate, intentional, and premeditated, with full awareness of profit to the doer and pain to the victim, it becomes an open sore to the community. Micah must have shouted loudly, "Woe to them that devise iniquity, and work evil upon their beds! when the morning is light, they practise it . . . they covet fields, and take them by violence; and houses, and take them away: . . . they oppress a man . . . and his heritage" (2:1–2).

Open lawlessness was practiced by the bold transgressors who had little respect for human rights or moral values. Micah charged the people with sheer robbery as he said, "You strip the robe from the peaceful, from those who pass by trustingly with no thought of war" (2:8, RSV). Unsuspecting people, considering themselves perfectly safe as they traveled throughout the land, were attacked and looted as by an enemy army. The inference is that these robber gangs were hired by the wealthy to attack harmless travelers.

An accurate evaluation of a nation is found in her treatment of widows and children. Many years before James insisted that pure religion and undefiled is "to visit the fatherless and widows in their affliction" (1:27), Micah, who regarded the rising generation as the greatest asset a country possessed, delivered a special rebuke to those whose greed led them to dispossess widows and make children homeless. This treatment caused many of them to be sold as slaves, thus making them no longer citizens of the nation. Frederick Carl Eiselen says, "Their glory was their citizenship in the nation of Jehovah. When they were sold as slaves, they were cut off from the nation and thus they lost a privilege and glory belonging to them."

Perhaps the worst offense of the people was that they had engaged so ruthlessly in these practices that they had become spiritually insensitive and had lost all sense of moral distinction. They were no longer able to recognize justice. They had hated the good and loved the evil so completely that they had become emotionally incapable of even desiring to do good. Much has been written about an "unpardonable sin," but this seems to be a condition which is unpardonable. This is true, not because God will not forgive even the worst of sins, but because repentance is a prerequisite to forgiveness, and these people had become so evil that they had not the slightest desire for righteousness and ethical conduct.

Because the cities were built with blood and iniquity (3:10), the officials accepted bribes for favorable judgments, and the religious leaders performed merely for monetary gain, yet were comfortably certain that God was the nation's unconditional ally (3:11), there was but one word to be said to the people. Micah said it (3:12). The city would be plowed like a field. Even the mountain upon which the Temple sat would be forsaken and turned into a jungle. Because he was full of God's power, Micah had no alternative. He must declare to the nation the judgment that was coming because of their sin.

God's Goal in History (4–5)

Although in the first section of his prophecy Micah denounced Judah's sin and warned of judgment and immediate destruction, he was no mere prophet of doom. He lifted his eyes to the future and saw "the latter days" with all their glory in order to gain inspiration for present-day living and service.

Men's vision for the future always determines the quality of their immediate task. In every generation there have been those who condemn Christianity as being too "other worldly" in its emphasis. C. S. Lewis says, however, that history records that the Christians who have done most for the present world were those who thought most of the next world. "It is since Christians have largely ceased to think of the other world that they have become so ineffective in this. Aim at heaven and you will get earth thrown in; aim to earth, and you will get neither."

Micah's description of the ideal Jerusalem (4:1–3) is so strikingly similar to Isaiah's (2:1–4) that scholars have speculated at length on who is quoting the other. Perhaps the more logical explanation is that each is quoting an unknown prophet. These words represent a prophecy which had existed in the hearts of Israel for centuries—their dream of a world to come. "It shall come to pass in the latter days that the mountain of the house of the Lord shall be established as the highest of the mountains, and shall be raised up above the hills; and peoples shall flow to it, and many nations shall come, and say: 'Come, let us go up to the mountain of the

Lord, to the house of the God of Jacob; that he may teach us his ways and we may walk in his paths.' For out of Zion shall go forth the law, and the word of the Lord from Jerusalem. He shall judge between many peoples, and shall decide for strong nations afar off; and they shall beat their swords into plowshares, and their spears into pruning hooks; nation shall not lift up sword against nation, neither shall they learn war any more" (Micah 4:1–3, RSV). Micah's description of the golden age to come contains more than Isaiah's. He adds, "They shall sit every man under his vine and under his fig tree, and none shall make them afraid" (v. 4, RSV).

The true prophet in every generation sees beyond the limits of his own day to the time when the glory of God shall be as the waters that cover the sea. Abraham, even in the midst of idolatry, had a vision of what would be and, though discouraged because of the difficulty, "looked for a city which hath foundations, whose builder and maker is God" (Heb. 11:10). Although John on Patmos was overcome by the iniquity of Rome seated on her seven hills and drunk with the blood of Christians, he saw through that city to "the holy city, new Jerusalem, coming down from God out of heaven, prepared as a bride adorned for her husband" (Rev. 21:2). Even while his country was torn apart by civil war and strife, John Bright lifted the eyes of his countrymen to the glory of the peace and unity which might be and must be, insisting, "It may be but a vision, but I will cherish it."

Micah soon saw that national Israel, of itself, could not attain the goal. It would be necessary for God to discipline and purify his people through captivity in a foreign land. From the remnant, however, would come the strength to carry on God's work in the future. The prophet says the Lord will "gather those who have been driven away, and those whom I have afflicted; and the lame I will make the remnant; and those who were cast off, a strong nation" (4:6–7, RSV).

As he looks to the future, Micah sees even more. The remnant, unaided, cannot accomplish the task. It will require a strong personal leader, a ruler who can minister in the name of Jehovah to the spiritual needs of the people. Only such a man can bring peace and raise up an abundance of leaders to assure the nation's security. Regardless of any contemporary application that Micah's words (5:2–5) may have had for his own day, the promise finds its ultimate fulfilment only in Jesus of Nazareth.

There is a significant difference in Micah's concept and that of Isaiah concerning the Messiah. Both saw a golden age in the future, but each gave a different emphasis concerning it. To Isaiah, the golden age would be ushered in by an ideal ruler who would have all the grandeur and majesty of a towering personality and upon whose shoulders the government would rest. He would be, in the literal Hebrew words "a wonder of a counsellor, a hero of a God, a father of eternity and a prince of peace" (Isa. 9:6). The increase of his government would know no end. To Micah, however, the emphasis was quite different. He turned from the city with all of its pomp and prestige and saw a humble rural village. David had come from a small town, not from the big city. Likewise, the greatest Son of David would come from such a village. In fact, in God's amazing providence, it would, indeed, be the city of David, even Bethlehem.

Perhaps the greatest example of predictive prophecy to be found in the Old Testament is Micah's description of the birthplace of the future spiritual leader of the nation. Even the pre-existence of the Messiah is suggested as Micah adds, "whose goings forth have been from of old, from everlasting" (5:2). This interpretation may read too much into Micah's words, but at least, they may be understood to mean that the work of the coming ruler will be in accord with the eternal purposes of God.

The closing part of Micah's vision for the future portrays the spiritual remnant becoming God's instrument for spreading the principles of true righteousness to all the nations. The prophet pictures the remnant "in the midst of many peoples like dew from the Lord" (5:7, RSV) and also "among the nations, in the midst of many peoples, like a lion among the beasts of the forest" (5:8, RSV).

The picture of Israel as dew is one of the most striking metaphors in the Old Testament. To the simple, nonscientific mind of the Hebrew, the production of dew on a clear night was a completely divine work. He had no concept of secondary causes in the natural sciences. His creative imagination poetically found in this phenomenon the fit symbol for the silent, life-giving influences from heaven that refreshed and made alive thirsty and withering souls. Where dew fell the parched vegetation lifted its drooping head. Hosea had said Jehovah will "be as the dew unto Israel" (14:5). His life-giving touch would cause Israel to blossom as the lily and his beauty to be as the olive tree. Now, Micah says, Israel will be as dew to the nations of the world. Perhaps the most significant aspect of the working of dew is its quietness. This, too, has always been the chief characteristic of the Saviour's work. Phillips Brooks in "Little Town of Bethlehem" says,

> How silently, how silently
> The wondrous gift is given
> So God imparts to human hearts
> The blessings of His heaven.

John Greenleaf Whittier prayed in "Dear Lord and Father of Mankind,"

> Drop thy still dews of quietness
> Till all our strivings cease.

The final part of this messianic section (5:8–15) may seem the least applicable to the present, but closer study will show it to be most relevant. The prophet describes the spiritual remnant as a lion among the beasts of the forest. The closing verses picture the sins of the land being stamped out by the power of God. The witchcrafts, graven images, and other elements of corrupt worship will be destroyed.

How will all this be done? Apparently it will be crushed by the avenging hand of a punitive God as he sends the military might of a foreign invader. This, from the viewpoint of secular history, was done.

However, there seems to be a deeper meaning. The gospel has power to change the individual *and* society. Every great triumph of social righteousness has been the result, directly or indirectly, of the preaching of the gospel. Richard Green, with his sociological concepts, did not transform the slums of East London. He tried and failed. William Booth and his wife Catherine, preaching the saving and transforming power of the gospel, had much greater success.

This message of Micah is relevant for our most urgent problem—the matter of personal relationship. Preaching on world brotherhood and urging men to love one another is not the most effective way of dealing with this problem. James Stewart in *The Strong Name* insists that this is approaching the task from the wrong end. He suggests that the toil and energy now being put into effort to promote world brotherhood on a natural basis should be turned into another channel. Stewart says, "Suppose you bring men face to face with God in Christ. Suppose they feel the impact of Jesus, and come under the spell of Jesus. Why then, the other thing we are after, the brotherhood we long for, begins to come in of its own accord. It comes as a by-product. And thus the problem solves itself."

Although men realize the impossibility of complete world brotherhood based on Christian principles until Jesus comes again, it remains a part of Christian purpose. The question is not one of preaching either personal salvation or social progress. Both are a part of the same gospel. The new birth comes first, and redeemed men will produce a new world.

What Does God Want? (6–8)

The last section of Micah's prophecy gathers up the threads and weaves them together into a comprehensive summary. Words already spoken are affirmed, but the emphasis in this section is on the content of true religion. Many scholars say that the greatest single statement of the Old Testament is found in Micah's words, "What does the Lord require of you but to do justice, and to love kindness, and to walk humbly with your God?" (6:8, RSV).

The section opens with a literary vehicle which attracts immediate attention. It is in the form of a debate between God and the people. George Adam Smith says, "The heart must be dull that does not leap to the Presences before which the trial is enacted."

After a preliminary statement that the Lord has a controversy with Israel and a challenge to the people to state their case, the Lord, through his prophet, asks a soul-searching question: "What have I done to you? In what have I wearied you? Answer me!" (6:3, RSV). He then reminds them of the great deliverance from Egypt and the accompanying providences. He concludes by giving the reason for these favors, "that you may know the saving acts of the Lord" (6:5, RSV).

Judged by any standard, verses 6–8 are the heart of the book. Micah presents the plea of the people in forensic form: How shall they come before the Lord? Shall they come with burnt offerings? Will the Lord be pleased with the gifts of their hands? Would thousands of rams or ten thousand rivers of oil satisfy him? This question is as old as religion itself. Micah's answer is unsurpassed. God will not accept the works of man's hands in lieu of the devotion of his heart. The prophet, having spoken for the people, now speaks for God. "He has showed you, O man, what is good; and what does the Lord require of you but to do justice, and to love kindness, and to walk humbly with your God?" (6:8, RSV). This is the essence of true religion in every generation. This is God's desire for all who worship him.

In this statement, Micah summarizes the message of his three eighth-century contemporaries. The theme of Amos was justice. He pled, "Let justice roll down like waters, and righteousness like an everflowing stream" (Amos 5:24, RSV). The theme of Hosea was love, and the Hebrew word "hsedh" used by Micah and translated "kindness," was Hosea's word for love or "mercy." The expression "walk humbly with your God" speaks of Isaiah's concept of fellowship with the Lord. To Isaiah, God's greatest characteristic was his holiness. He is the Holy One of Israel. If man walks with God, he must approach him in humility and have fellowship with him as an obedient child. Micah gathers up the three into a definitive statement concerning the eternal demand of God. Religion begins, of course, with a redemptive relationship with God, but it is not complete until the love produced by this relationship has overflowed to become concern for the welfare of one's fellow beings. Religion without this humanistic touch is empty and without meaning. It is equally futile without daily fellowship with God that is completely free from pride.

Then Micah's sublime definition of true religion was followed by a bitter denunciation of the people's conduct, especially those in the cities. Speaking through Micah, the Lord asks, "Shall I acquit the man with wicked scales and with a bag of deceitful weights?" (6:11, RSV). Micah declares "The good man is perished out of the earth: and there is none upright" (7:2). Both the prince and the judge ask for bribes (7:3), and they all lie in wait for blood as each person hunts his brother with a net (7:2). The dishonesty of the land not only turned neighbor against neighbor and friend against friend, but it had invaded the homes and turned members of the family against each other. No one can trust anyone! Micah says, "The best of them is as a brier: the most upright is sharper than a thorn hedge" (7:4).

What will be the result of such a condition? The people shall be made desolate because of their sins. They shall eat but not be satisfied; put away but not save; sow but not reap; tread olives but not annoint themselves with oil; tread grapes but not drink wine (6:14–15). They shall be made a desolation and be scorned by others. They will sit in darkness bearing the indignation of the Lord because they have sinned against him.

Micah closes with a promise for the future. Although Israel falls, she shall rise. The enemies who gloat over Israel's downfall shall see her restoration and shall be ashamed because they doubted the power of God. They shall lick the dust like a serpent. They shall turn in fear to the God of Israel.

The closing verses summarize a great truth. The Hebrew word "Micah" means literally, "Who is like thee?" The prophet makes a word play on his own name and asks, "Who is a God like thee?" What is it that makes God so incomparable? He is the One who forgives sin and retains a remnant for himself and his purposes.

The relevance of Micah for this day is that God demands the highest and the best, but he is merciful toward those who are weak. He is gracious toward those who are sinners. He will not retain his anger forever but will cast all men's sins into the depth of the sea (7:18–19). If Micah were preaching today, he would shout with the hymn writer, "My God, How Great Thou Art!"

5

Sin Betrays
(ZEPHANIAH)

A man who was slightly deficient in formal education was discussing a friend. He remarked, "The trouble with him is he is lacking in ignichative." He meant to say that his friend was lacking in initiative, but the word he coined is quite provocative.

Many people have no fire, not even a spark. They seem utterly incapable of igniting anything or anybody. They seem to lack the capacity to become aroused at injustice or to blaze with anger when confronted by wickedness in high places. They also seem emotionally incapable of being enthusiastic concerning some great endeavor. In short, they have no "ignichative."

Of course passion out of hand can produce a cyclone of devastating results. A temper tantrum, lust of the flesh, or love of money, invites self-destruction comparable to a five-alarm fire. Earl Douglas reminds us, however, that a "life with no spark in it, no illumination, no capacity to flare up into anger over hateful injustices, constitutes drabness almost equivalent to death itself."

The book of Zephaniah contains the message of a man who

was cognizant of Judah's sin and burned passionately as he saw certain destruction because of her trangression. Sanford Yoder, the Mennonite scholar, calls Zephaniah "the orator, a man of straightforward speech, severe and uncompromising in his denunciation of the evils of his day and the sins of his countrymen."

As for the man himself, Zephaniah's ancestry is traced back four generations to Hezekiah. Since it is very unusual to find in the Old Testament an ancestry traced past two generations, there is strong reason for believing that the "Hezekiah" of Zephaniah's genealogy must have been a notable person— probably the king. The word "Zephaniah" means "Jehovah hides," and could well refer to his being born during the period when Manasseh shed innocent blood by killing any who tended to champion the cause of righteousness. Perhaps Zephaniah's parents, being godly people, were forced to hide their son for his safety.

Most scholars believe that Zephaniah was reared in the city of Jerusalem. His book indicates in some places an exception- ally accurate knowledge of the city. Some think he was harsh, without compassion and unsympathetic. This is not quite fair to the prophet. He *was* a proclaimer of judgment, but his message was interspersed with words of tenderness and hope for the future.

The time of Zephaniah's ministry is fairly well circum- scribed. He preached during the reign of Josiah. Since he condemned the sins of the land which were abolished forcibly by the king in the reformation of 621 B.C., he must have preached before that event. Probably he is best assigned to the period contemporary with Jeremiah's entrance into the prophetic ministry, about 626 B.C. At this time the Scythians were carrying on raiding expeditions in the area and part of the book seems to have been written against this background.

This prophet has one theme—judgment for sin. He "hits the ground running" as he opens the book with a declaration of certain retribution for transgression and iniquity. This judgment will be cataclysmic in nature. He shouts, "I will utterly sweep away everything from the face of the earth. . . I will sweep away man and beast . . . the birds of the air and the fish of the sea. I will overthrow the wicked; I will cut off mankind from the face of the earth" (1:2–3, RSV). Judah and Jerusalem must pay for their sins (1:1 to 2:3). The nations round about must likewise suffer the same consequence (2:3 to 3:8). Then he looks beyond the hopeless condition of the present to see a glorious future for those who turn to God and seek his statutes (3:9–20).

Punishments (1:1 to 2:3)

As Zephaniah surveyed Jerusalem and Judah he saw a discouraging situation. Baal worshipers and priests of the Lord had so blended their activities that true worship had become virtually impossible to distinguish from the counterfeit. People were gathered on the housetops worshiping the stars. Rulers of Judah who had pledged themselves to uphold the faith of Jehovah were arraying themselves in foreign dress and mimicking all kinds of pagan customs. Some had turned from following the Lord, others had never followed him at all. Like wine which has been undisturbed until it has thickened, the people had settled "on their lees" with a sickening sweet attitude of—"The Lord will do nothing. He will not do good—but neither will he harm. He is too much of a loving God to punish."

The prophet saw but one conclusion. Judah must be dealt with by the One against whom the people had sinned. Although they had accumulated much wealth, it would become a spoil for the enemy. Although they had built houses, they would not dwell in them. Although they had planted vineyards, they would not drink the wine from them. The nation had lost its sense of right and wrong. No longer did it feel shame for its deeds. Such a people must be punished!

What form will the judgment take? With horrifying abruptness Zephaniah warned that the same outstretched hand which delivered the nation from Egyptian bondage would be stretched out again, but this time for another purpose—to make the entire land a desolation and a waste. The "noise of a cry from the fish gate," the "wailing from the new part of town," and the "crashing from the hills"—destruction and devastation would be thorough and all-inclusive. The inhabitants of Maktesh will wail, the people of Canaan will be undone, and the people laden with silver will be cut off.

Nowhere else in the Old Testament is the day of the Lord presented in more emphatic terms—a day of wrath, trouble, distress, wasteness, desolation, darkness, gloominess, clouds, thick darkness! A day when the trumpet of alarm shall be sounded against the fortified cities and defense towers! A day when the Lord will bring such distress upon the people that they shall walk as blind men! Their blood shall be poured out as dust! Their flesh shall be like garbage! The whole land shall be devoured as fire! All who dwell in the land shall have a speedy and terrible end! All of this, according to Zephaniah, was because they had sinned against the Lord!

Although the prophet did not mention by name the instrument of the Lord's chastisement, some scholars believe that he referred to the Scythians who were nearby at the time of his preaching. There is a striking similarity between this section and Jeremiah 4:5 to 6:30. Both messages are believed to have been delivered against the same historical background. Babylon was the nation which actually fulfilled these warnings after the Scythians passed off the scene. Probably when Zephaniah uttered his words of coming judgment, he had in mind the Scythians whom John Skinner in *Prophecy and Religion* describes as "a wild primeval, hyperborean race of uncouth speech, cruel and pitiless, moving on horseback, armed with bow and spear, sweeping like a tornado over the land and leaving desolation in their tracks, prowling like hungry wolves or howling leopards round the fenced cities where the terrified inhabitants have taken refuge." It is no wonder Zephaniah spoke with alarm and urgency as he warned the people of God's chastening hand.

There is good reason to believe that the Lord withheld punishment because of the people's repentance. Zephaniah probably preached about 626 or 625 B.C. In 621 B.C. an ancient law book was discovered in the Temple. When it was read, reforms were established in the land and a period of righteous living followed. Later, this reform movement became more nationalistic than spiritual and failed to effect permanent results, but the "great reformation," did grant a temporary immunity from this judgment. It came a few years later than Zephaniah prophesied in his urgent message, but it was every bit as devastating as he predicted.

Parallels (2:4 to 3:8)

Having declared Jerusalem's fate in unmistakable words, Zephaniah's prophecy dealt with countries round about Judah. Not all the nations were mentioned, but the prophet pronounced against enemies on the east, west, south, and north.

S. L. Edgar says it is fair to assume that the prophet meant for those named to be representative of all who oppose God or God's people and who are, therefore, under judgment.

Why would Zephaniah include a section like this in a message to the people of Judah? Probably there are two reasons, either of which would be sufficient. First, all people everywhere are subject to the moral law of sin and retribution, regardless of any revelation of God's nature and character they may have received. Second, there is an element of comfort for Judah in certain words of this section as she is assured that a remnant shall possess the places the enemy left bare by God's judgment.

The Philistines are dealt with first by the prophet. Four of the five major cities (Gaza, Ashkelon, Ashdod, Ekron) are called by name. Gath is not mentioned. It may be that by this time it had been destroyed or humbled to a position of relative unimportance. According to Zephaniah, the entire territory of this people who live on the western seacoast of Canaan would be uprooted. Every word uttered deepens the gloom of the terrible pronouncement. The fertility of the land would be cursed. James Wolfendale says, "This once fertile tract by the sea, thickly dotted with the crowded hives of human industry . . . shepherds will dig it up to build their huts and shelter their flocks."

The suddenness of the oncoming judgment is emphasized in the declaration to Ashdod. "They shall drive out Ashdod at the noon day" (2:4). Most scholars believe that the phrase indicates the suddenness of the city's fall while the men were resting and not expecting an attack. A. B. Davidson suggests that it may refer to a storming of the city by sheer and open force, a possible allusion, by way of contrast, to the siege of

Ashdod by Psamtik I which lasted twenty-nine years and was actually in progress while Zephaniah's words were being spoken. Frederick Carl Eiselen, however, provides the most interesting and plausible interpretation of this expression. He suggests that the city will be captured after merely a brief assault lasting only from morning until noon. He points out a similar expression in an inscription of Esarhaddon, king of Assyria, "Memphis . . . I took in the half of the day." Eiselen says "at noonday; here also the emphasis seems to be on the brevity of time in which the city was taken."

Not only the suddenness but the thoroughness of the destruction is emphasized. So completely will the cities be destroyed that no one will be left. Zephaniah warned, "Woe unto the inhabitants of the sea coast. . . I will even destroy thee, that there shall be no inhabitant" (2:5).

The enemies of Israel to the east were Moab and Ammon. These people, who were descendants of the incestuous relationship between Lot and his daughters (Gen. 19:30-38), were characterized by two besetting sins. First, they, especially Moab, were a people of great pride. Jeremiah said, "We have heard the pride of Moab, (he is exceedingly proud) his loftiness, and his arrogancy, and his pride, and the haughtiness of his heart" (48:29). Zephaniah speaks of both nations as people of pride who have reproached Israel and magnified themselves against her border. Their second characteristic sin was that they constantly and presumptuously violated the boundaries of Israel and attempted to seize and annex her territory. This old charge against the Ammonites dated back to the days of Amos who said, "They have ripped up the women with child of Gilead, that they might enlarge their border" (1:13). Whenever it was at all

possible, Moab also passed the frontier into Israel and took
territory belonging to Reuben and Gad, according to inscriptions on the Moabite Stone.

Two fates are pronounced for those countries to the east of
Judah. They would suffer the same destruction as Sodom and
Gomorrah had, absorption by Israel. Zephaniah foretold their
becoming "a land possessed by nettles and salt pits, and a
waste for ever. The remnant of my people shall plunder them,
and the survivors of my nation shall possess them" (2:9, RSV).
Clyde Francisco calls special attention to the declaration that
the Lord will "famish all the gods of the earth" (2:11). Usually
the prophets spoke of the destruction of false gods, but here
they will be made lean. The Lord will prove himself to be the
one true God with such effectiveness that he will take away
the loyalty and gifts of others to their gods. Thus, these false
gods will become lean and starve to death.

In the oracles against Moab and Ammon the prophet has
dealt with west and east, half of the foreign foes. South and
north remain. The superiority of the Lord God in his divine
warfare against all powers that seek to usurp his authority
is clearly emphasized. Rebellion against God's sovereignty is
present in every generation. God assures men that he will
be victorious.

The prophetic word against the southern foe is brief. Many
scholars think Ethiopia, against whom the oracle is directed,
stands for Egypt. For a brief period Ethiopia and Egypt were
united in government and the Ethiopian pharaohs actually
ruled the united empire. By the time of Zephaniah the Ethiopian rulers had been expelled. There may be other factors,
unknown because of lack of full information about Egyptian
history. It seems safe to conclude that Ethiopia stands for the
southern foes of Judah and the Lord.

The enemy to the north was Assyria whose capital was Nineveh. This nation was the personification of supreme self-confidence. She felt secure, believing that no rival existed that could threaten, or even question, her position. Beginning with Amos, all God's spokesmen looked upon Assyria as the divinely appointed agent, the "rod of God's anger" to execute judgment upon rebellious Israel. This nation, however, had surpassed its commission. Its cruel policies toward conquered peoples were contrary to God's will.

Zephaniah saw nothing but waste for Nineveh. This self-sufficient city, would become the resting place for animals. The mansions of the wealthy, the temples to pagan gods, the palace of the kings, the storehouses containing loot from conquered countries—all would be laid bare. The paneled walls and elaborate designs would be exposed to the elements of nature—storms, winds, and rains. All would become ruins —a dwelling place for pelicans and hedgehogs. Careless living produced the situation which made this divine judgment necessary. Assyria was unaware of her need for God. Such an attitude always results in careless living and, eventually, defiance of God's moral laws. Although Assyria rejoiced tumultuously and, in self-satisfied security, boisterously celebrated her triumphs, regarding herself as invincible, she will meet the inevitable fate of all who ignore God's ethical exactions, moral demands, and spiritual imperatives.

Having dealt with God's enemies in the nations round about, the prophet then turned his attention to the enemy within the gates of the city. Men with little light and limited revelation will be punished, but those with much light and fuller revelation have greater guilt and greater condemnation.

Jerusalem was God's city, and the inhabitants were his people in a unique way. The whole community had become corrupt, but the rottenness was most evident among the civic and spiritual leaders.

Princes and judges, like roaring lions, were constantly lusting for new victims. Prophets and priests used their offices for personal gain rather than for instructing the people in God's standard of integrity and justice. The Lord's warning that he dwells in the midst of his people and will send correction for this corruption had fallen on deaf ears.

This section closes with a plea for the people to realize God's determination to adjust all things in harmony with his holiness of character. All enemies of God will be overthrown. Man cannot flaunt God forever. Righteousness will be vindicated and victorious. This truth is the concluding and comforting thought of the final section of Zephaniah's prophecies.

Promises (2:9–20)

There is a great difference between Bible pessimism and secular pessimism. The Bible is realistic in all areas of human life. The prophets never glossed over the sinfulness of human nature nor the suffering which comes as an inevitable result of wrongdoing. In places they describe human life and destiny as bleak and black as some cynical writers of contemporary literature. Raymond Calkins, however, makes this striking contrast, "In the latter case we are left there and in the former we are not."

One unique feature of the prophets is that through their most somber and austere messages a ray of light shines and a note of hope is heard. Even in the most discouraging days, the prophets believed implicitly that evil would be overthrown and God's cause would be victorious. What motivation for men today if they shared the prophets' confidence and optimism!

Few prophets had an outlook darker than Zephaniah's at the beginning. Yet, the blackness of his night progressively gives way to the gleams of dawn. The last section (3:9–20) emerges into the full light of day. Although wickedness may corrupt society and poison the streams of morality, an indestructible remnant of God's people remain and are renewed to become the seed from which new life shall come forth. One can have confidence in this sublime truth and, even in the midst of a disordered world, find meaning and purpose in life.

The fire of the Lord's jealousy consumes, but it also purifies. God's will on earth must be done by people of pure lips, that is, people who serve him in sincerity and in truth. Clyde Francisco is intrigued by the expression "pure lips." At Babel, men's tongues were confounded. At Pentecost, each man heard the gospel in his own tongue. Here in Zephaniah is the transition between the two. Zephaniah paved the way for Pentecost.

Zephaniah recognized that a new world order must be made up of converted mankind. Possibly, in this final section is the New Testament doctrine of regeneration in embryo. Zephaniah pictured God exterminating the proud and haughty and leaving a people who "seek refuge in the name of the Lord" (3:12, RSV). This remnant "shall not do iniquity, nor speak lies; neither shall a deceitful tongue be found in their mouth: for they shall feed and lie down, and none shall make them afraid" (3:13). Earlier in the book, Zephaniah followed his prophecy of the nation's certain punishment with the invitation: "Seek ye the Lord, all ye meek of the earth . . . it may be ye shall be hid in the day of the Lord's anger" (2:3). Although fear of God's wrath is not the highest motive, it should not be discarded as an incentive to turn from sin and become a new creature.

The book of Zephaniah closes with rejoicing as hope replaces gloomy foreboding. The redeemed of the land will enjoy the rich blessing of God's presence. The Lord has pardoned. He has broken the encircling power of the enemies round about his people. The darkness of gloom and doom has given way to the radiant light of God's grace. One great conviction undergirds the prophet's certainty. The living God is in the midst of his people. This idea finds full consummation in the New Testament doctrine of the incarnation—Emmanuel—God with us. Charles Kingsley once wrote, "I am struggling through infinite darkness and chaos by means of one bright pathway which I find to be the only explanation of a thousand mysteries, I mean the Incarnation of our Lord." This hope is our hope—indeed it is our only hope—for today's world.

As long as sin and suffering exist, Zephaniah's book is relevant and essential. As long as man fights the battle against wickedness in high places and wonders if the struggle is worthwhile, as long as God's people are lonely in an unfriendly world, as long as proud men crush humble souls, as long as men look to the future wonderingly and fearfully, wanting to trust completely but needing assurance from God, as long as they tremblingly ask with Judah's last king, "Is there a word from the Lord?" Zephaniah's oratorical masterpiece will bring assurance and conviction for the living of these days.

6

Enduring Love
(HOSEA)

In the *Vicar of Wakefield*, Oliver Goldsmith asks:

> When lovely woman stoops to folly,
>   And finds too late that men betray,
> What charm can soothe her melancholy?
>   What art can wash her guilt away?
>
> The only art her guilt to cover,
>   To hide her shame from every eye,
> To give repentance to her lover,
>   And wring his bosom, is—to die.

But God is not like that! Isaiah said, "Though your sins be as scarlet, they shall be as white as snow; though they be red like crimson, they shall be as wool" (1:18). To one taken in the very act of adultery, Jesus said, "Neither do I condemn thee: go, and sin no more" (John 8:11).

Hosea's tenderness supplements the harsh and blunt message of Amos. The two were among the first writing prophets. Although they were virtually historical contemporaries, their message and style differed greatly. Amos saw outward conduct. Hosea saw the inward motivation. Amos demanded justice and righteousness. Hosea believed that love was the key to every problem. Amos came from the solitude of the wilds and was a "loner"; Hosea found his greatest inspiration in the company of people he loved. Amos' ministry was brief. Hosea's lasted nearly half a century.

The book of Hosea is unusual and difficult to analyze and absorb. It contains the substance of the prophet's fervent and recurring appeals as he sought to call sinful Israel back to her God. On the surface the book appears dull, but deeper study produces spiritual blessings. The average person reading through the book finds little more than a few isolated verses which often are made "proof text" expressions of truth.

The prophet's message came out of the sensitive soul of a man who had suffered greatly. Because the book holds an unusual amount of emotion, it has been called a "succession of sobs" and a "diary of a soldier at the front in the midst of battle." The fetters of grammar often limited Hosea's deep feeling. Images and thoughts pursue one another, making the content difficult to outline. The book is torn with agony and is one of the saddest books in the Bible. It has been called "The Lamentations of Jehovah."

As a man, Hosea is an interesting subject for study. His name means "salvation," and the Hebrew word is similar to Joshua and Jesus. Hosea was the son of Beeri, but nothing is known of his family. All that is known of Hosea is learned from his book. Scholars are virtually certain he was from the Northern Kingdom. Occasionally he spoke to Judah, but the special interest and burden of his message was to Israel. He demonstrated a remarkable knowledge of the topography of Israel. Ewald says, "Every sentence of Hosea makes us feel that he had not merely once upon a time made this kingdom a passing visit, as Amos did, but knows it with the inmost consciousness of his heart, and follows all its deeds and efforts and fortunes with the emotions of such a profound sympathy as is only conceivable in the case of a native-born prophet of the country." George Adam Smith notes, "The poetry of Hosea clings about his native soil like its trailing vines. . . . Hosea's love steals across his whole land like the dew, provoking every separate scent and color till all Galilee lies before us lustrous and fragrant."

Apparently Hosea was familiar with the cities of Israel, but his thorough acquaintance with the terminology of farm life indicates his rural background. Laetsch observes, "Most of Hosea's symbols are connected with agriculture, rural life. He may have been a tiller of the soil before he was called as a prophet. His intimate knowledge of the history of his people and the political affairs of his day, the language, which, while terse, is beautiful, containing many similes, references, and figures which only a cultured man would employ, seem to point to the wealthier class of the rural communities."

The time of Hosea's ministry is given as "in the days of Uzziah, Jotham, Ahaz, and Hezekiah, kings of Judah, and in the days of Jeroboam the son of Joash, king of Israel" (1:1). The cumulative total of these reigns would be about 140 years. The general verdict of scholarship places his period of ministry between 40 and 45 years. The latter part of the reign of Jeroboam II forms the background for the first three chapters of Hosea. Chapters 4 to 14 reflect the chaotic period following Jeroboam's death until the fall of Israel in 722 B.C. Thus, Hosea has been called the "Prophet of the Decline and Fall of the Northern Kingdom."

The general condition of that day was noisy, sinful, and chaotic. It was a time of political change and confusion. Tiglath-pileser came into power in Assyria in 745 B.C. and he began a military campaign westward. Outside Israel, the plundering invader was loose. Inside, anarchy was present. Politically, Jeroboam II was Israel's strongest ruler. When he died, a period of changing kings followed. Zechariah reigned six months and was killed. Shallum lasted only one month. Of the last six kings in Israel Menahem was the only one who died a natural death. Pekahiah reigned two years and was assassinated by Pekah who was put to death by a Syrian conspiracy. Hoshea then ruled until the captivity. The picture of these times is of one king on the throne and another trying to get there.

Lying diplomacy, social decay, and moral corruption were common. Evil was becoming more entrenched. Class cleavage was increasing. The rich were becoming richer and the poor, poorer. The middle class, always the stabilizing group of any society, had all but disappeared. The courts were corrupt. Family life had decayed. Violence was abroad in the land as "blood touched blood." The priests were the leading defenders of the status quo. They had organized to keep people in sin rather than to save them from sin. This situation augmented their income. Religious degeneracy and idolatrous superstition were prevalent. Much formal religion existed but no heartfelt spirituality. The people flocked to places of worship on the festival days then returned to their old sins. They feigned repentance in order to get the sun to shine, then returned to their same iniquities. Hosea's voice was the last word to a nation headed for catastrophe.

A Look at the Book

In Hosea's writings must be recognized a twofold division. Chapters 1 through 3 tell of the domestic tragedy in the prophet's life. Chapters 4 through 14 tell of Hosea's ministry during the chaotic period of Israel's last days. George Adam Smith calls this section "the noise of a nation falling to pieces, the crumbling of a splendid past." The last eleven chapters of the book are difficult to outline. There seem to be four main sections.

The first section (4:1 to 6:3) contains an indictment against the nation. The last three verses are an invitation to return to the Lord. This section was probably delivered during the earlier part of Hosea's ministry. The second section (6:4 to 10:15) contains a second discourse. An invitation to repentance is included in the last few verses of this section also. This oracle seems to be related to the latter days of Hosea's ministry, near the end of the nation's history. Indeed, the invitation to repentance seems almost to presuppose its rejection. The third section (11:1-11) is a beautiful poem that reveals the fatherhood of God. It is perhaps the greatest single section in the book. The last section (11:12 to 14:9) is a final message to the decaying nation. An invitation to repentance—"love's final call"—is given once more at the conclusion. These three sections (4:1 to 6:3; 6:4 to 10:15; 11:12 to 14:9) possibly represent three distinct divisions in the ministry of Hosea as the sinful nation progressed in depravity and rushed headlong to doom. Such an outline as this makes the book of Hosea more meaningful than to divide it into many fragments with little or no continuity in message. This outline will be the basis for further examination of the main thoughts of the prophet's ministry.

Gospel Through Grief (1:1-21; 3:1-5)

As Hosea surveyed his past life, he realized that his ministry began when God told him to take Gomer as his wife. In this marriage relationship and the events which followed were truths which Hosea must receive in order to preach effectively and meaningfully to Israel. Experience is the best, and in reality, the only teacher.

What kind of person was Gomer? Without reviewing the various theories, one fact must be accepted as final: The moral problem is too great and the analogy to Israel's history is destroyed if the assumption is made that God commanded Hosea to marry a woman who was impure at the time of the wedding. The best interpretation of "Go, take unto thee a wife of whoredoms and children of whoredoms" is that the young girl had a background of pagan religion and was inclined toward sensual attractions of life. Although she was morally pure and a virgin at the time of her wedding, she followed her tendencies and became an adulteress or perhaps a temple prostitute shortly after the marriage. This story is a warning to God's young prophets today to be cautious about choosing a helpmate with too much social ambition and love for the worldly things.

When a child was born, Hosea surveyed the historical situation and gave the child a symbolic name. The time had come for God's pronounced judgment upon the house of Jehu to be executed. The name "Jezreel" was a reminder to the people of God's active presence in Israel's history. There is doubt as to the paternity of the second and third child. Of Jezreel the writer said, "She bare him a son." Of the other two he merely says, "She bare a daughter" and "She bare a son." Their symbolic names were significant also, especially the last. The daughter's name Lo-ruhamah means "no mercy" and signified the rapidly closing door of opportunity for Israel. The third child was named Lo-ammi which means "not my people" or "none of mine." Scholars are virtually certain that this last name referred not only to Israel's apostasy but also to Gomer's infidelity.

A man usually finds his earthly heaven or hell in the woman he marries. Gomer did not share the burden of her husband's ministry. Hosea was concerned about his nation. He knew Israel's "Indian summer" of prosperity was about to give way to the winter of judgment. He could hear the rumble of Assyria's war chariots and spent day and night pleading with the people. Gomer, like Gallio, "cared for none of these things."

One day tragedy struck. Perhaps it occurred like this: Hosea came home as usual, but something was different. The children were huddled by the door, tired and hungry. The house had a deserted look. The fire was out. Although he was tired, he began in a clumsy masculine way to prepare the meal. He was not skilled in this and blundered through the task. Eventually, however, the children were quieted and he hurried them to bed.

In the loneliness of the room Hosea now had time to think. He was too sick of heart to touch his food. The suspicions Hosea had carried in his sensitive soul now leaped out before him as mocking specters. A noise at the door gave him momentary hope, but it was short lived. A neighbor had come to pass on the gossip. Gomer was seen leaving with a man. With a laugh she had bidden someone to tell her old man she was through with him and his narrow-minded mediocrity. Hosea's world crashed in that moment. He asked the neighbor to leave him alone. He staggered over to the smoldering fire. How like his own life it was! Only ashes and embers remained!

Perhaps he sat gazing into the fire until the gray dawn began to filter into the room. It seemed like the beginning of an endless, hopeless day! Then a voice seemed to speak, "You loved Gomer, the bride of your youth! So Israel is my bride! Gomer has broken your heart. Israel has broken mine! Do you know now how I feel when she goes whoring after other lovers?"

Through his grief Hosea gained his gospel. His tears became telescopes. He saw now the *true nature of sin.* It was not a mere violation of law. It was severance of relationship by broken vows of love. He saw the *essence of religion.* A man wants more in a wife than someone to cook meals, wash dishes, and keep the house clean. He wants companionship. God wants more from his people than the performance of the perfunctories, obedience to the externals of legalized religious requirements. He wants man to live in intimate fellowship with him and know the joy of love, mercy, and righteousness. Hosea saw the *heart of God.* Only when man has suffered can he understand God's suffering and his redemptive love. Sarah Williams writes:

> Is it so, O Christ in heaven,
> That the highest suffer most?
> That the strongest wander fartherest
> And are more hopelessly lost?
> That the mark of rank in nature
> Is capacity for pain
> That the anguish of the singer
> Means the sweetness of the strain? [1]

Yes, it is true. Hosea learned (in the words of Robert Browning Hamilton):

> I walked a mile with Sorrow
> And ne'er a word said she

> But oh the things I learned from her
> When Sorrow walked with me.[2]

How many years passed between chapter 1 and chapter 3 is not certain, but one day God spoke again to the prophet and told him to love this woman. He was divinely directed to the slave market where the derelicts of female humanity were being auctioned. God led his attention to one depraved woman. Hosea was startled! There was a slight resemblance between her and his wayward wife. He looked again! A tingling went throughout his body and a knot formed in his chest. Could this wreckage of womanhood possibly be his once pure bride? Undoubtedly! The wasted specimen standing before him was Gomer! The bidding started for her and Hosea knew in a moment why God had brought him here. The price of a slave was thirty pieces of silver (Ex. 21:32). Hosea had to supplement his fifteen shekels with a portion of barley, but he paid the price and the slave was delivered to him. Once again God had taught Hosea of his love for Israel. God's gospel is redemption! Grace is greater than guilt, and sinful mankind can be forgiven because of God's compassionate heart! Nowhere else in the Old Testament is the message of Christ so clearly prefigured!

A Nation in Decay
(4:1–5:15; 6:4 to 10:11; 11:12 to 13:16)

Three oracles contain the indictment against Israel and reasons for her decline and fall. They contain dark pictures. Each division closes with an invitation to repentance, but only the evidences of a nation which had "lost its moorings and was adrift on a threatening sea" are dealt with here.

The sins of Israel were many. Hosea said, "There is no

truth, nor goodness, nor knowledge of God in the land. There
is nought but swearing and breaking faith, and killing, and
stealing, and committing adultery; they break out, and blood
toucheth blood" (4:1-2, ASV). The five participles are Hebrew infinitive absolutes—graphic and forceful. The expression
"blood toucheth blood" indicates violent bloodshed—evidence
of the instability and sinful rot which has been called the
"gangrene of the nation." In these three prophetic discourses
Hosea brings ten definite charges against the people:

1. They had *lost respect for authority.* "Yet let no man . . .
   reprove . . . for thy people are as they that strive with
   the priest" (4:4).
2. They were *completely ignorant of the true nature of
   God.* Hosea had in mind spiritual comprehension not intellectual learning when he declared, "My people are
   destroyed for lack of knowledge" (4:6).
3. They were *given over to their passions and lusts and
   bent on satisfying the lower elements of their nature.*
   Hosea must have shouted with horror, "Whoredom and
   wine . . . take away the understanding" (4:11, ASV);
   "they have played the harlot, departing from . . . their
   God" (4:12, ASV); "they have committed lewdness. In
   the house of Israel . . . a horrible thing: there whoredom is found" (6:9-10, ASV).
4. *The religious leaders had sold out to the situation.* The
   priests had become "a snare at Mizpah, and a net spread
   upon Tabor" (5:1, ASV). They were feeding upon the
   sin of the people and had their heart set on iniquity
   (4:8).
5. The people had become *caught in the vicious circle of
   sinfulness and were incapable even of desiring the good
   life.* Hosea summarized, "Their doings will not suffer

them to turn unto their God" (5:4, ASV). Phillips renders
it, "It is their deeds which block their pathway back to
God, For their spirit is steeped in unfaithfulness." [3]

6. Their *goodness was shallow* and their *repentance was
superficial.* "O Ephraim, what shall I do unto thee? . . .
for your goodness is as a morning cloud, and as the dew
that goeth early away" (6:4, ASV).

7. They had *lost their sense of uniqueness* because of their
identification with people of pagan practices. Israel was
a "trafficker" with the balances of deceit in his hand and
loving to oppress (12:7, ASV), as one who "mixeth himself among the peoples" (7:8, ASV). "Ephraim is joined
to idols: let him alone" (4:17).

8. They were *completely unconscious of their moral and
spiritual decay,* having become *lopsided in their spiritual
development.* "Ephraim is a cake not turned. Strangers
have devoured his strength, and he knoweth it not: yea,
gray hairs are here and there upon him, and he knoweth
it not" (7:8–9, ASV).

9. They had *left out God* and had *resorted to compensating
activities.* "Israel hath forgotten his Maker, and buildeth
temples" (8:14).

10. They had *continued in sin until it had become a way of
life.* "They are a crowd of drunkards given over to lust,
Loving their shameful worship more than my glory"
(4:18, Phillips). They had "plowed wickedness" and
"reaped iniquity" (10:13); they had "sinned from the
days of Gibeah" (10:9). "It is thy destruction, O Israel,
that thou art against me, against thy help" (13:9, ASV).

How discouraging is the picture! Sin had taken a tragic
toll. The fundamental failure of the nation was that she has
forgotten her God and, in selfish pride, had gone off after

other lovers. Hosea's experience with his unfaithful wife col-
ored all his messages. Each of the three indictments grew
progressively harsh and hopeless. For Israel repentance was
virtually impossible. The people had become incapable of
moral distinctions. Sin had cut the optic nerve of the soul.
Kyle Yates writes succinctly concerning Hosea's charges,
"What a keen observation! Spiritual perception is impossible.
The brain is clouded. The mind is weakened. The people
are utterly stupid. The power of moral appreciation is gone
completely. What a lesson for the people of any age . . . Sin
has brought about the inevitable destruction."

Two Pictures of God
(2:2–23; 11:1–11)

Through the "crisis of his own life situation" the prophet
came into personal encounter with God. Through this intimate
experience he gained insight into the true nature of Jehovah's
character. The twofold concept of God in his book was
gained through personal tragedy.

First, God is like a loving husband who is faithful to his
bride in spite of her infidelity (2:2–23). This metaphor was
used by later prophets but seems to have originated with
Hosea. Like Gomer, Israel had left her husband and played
the harlot. Jehovah had united himself to Israel in the wilderness. There he took her unto him as a bride. His choice of
Israel had been one of grace. Nothing in this slave people
claimed God's merit. How easily people who are redeemed
by grace forget their previous plight! Israel, like Gomer, went
after other lovers. She courted the affections of the pagan
gods, believing they could provide material necessities and
luxuries. Patiently, Jehovah waited by Israel even as Hosea

was long-suffering toward Gomer. The vigil was futile, however, and Israel, like Gomer, plunged rapidly to doom.

The loving husband was willing to believe that time would vindicate his faithful patience. He would speak to Israel and woo her with winsome words of love. His pleadings would be irresistible and she would return to her companion. Hosea expressed the heart of a loving husband, "I will betroth you to me for ever; I will betroth you to me in righteousness and in justice, in steadfast love, and in mercy. I will betroth you to me in faithfulness; and you shall know the Lord" (2:19–20, RSV).

When the bride is restored, a great transformation will take place. There will be peace in the land and righteousness will be restored to the people. Rather than judgment, the people will be "sown" unto their Lord. Where there has been "no mercy" there shall be an abundance of grace. The people who were declared to be illegitimate shall once more be God's people and he shall be their God.

> O to grace how great a debtor
> Daily I'm [we *all* are] constrained to be!

The other picture of God (11:1–11) is that of a loving father. R. E. Wolfe says, "It is understandable how one so devoted to his home was first to suggest that the relationship of Israel to the deity was like that of a son to father." Perhaps this revelation broke through to the prophet as he recalled earlier, happier days spent with his own children, teaching them to walk and steadying them as they took their first steps.

As the prophet faced the reality of the nation's sin and its inevitable result, he could hardly accept the certain consequence for Israel. "How shall I cast thee off, Israel? . . . my heart is turned within me, my compassions are kindled together" (11:8, ASV). The loving father made an all encompassing decison. He will not execute the fierceness of his wrath. He is God and not man. He is sovereign and free to choose. Although Israel is a prodigal child, the loving father can, in mercy forgive. This he will do!

The nation must be disciplined. But after the discipline of captivity, they shall return and once more be God's people and find their place in his purpose. This voice of exhaustless love reveals the riches of his grace and points to the Father's infinite and eternal work at Calvary where God showed man once and for all that he cannot and will not give up his creation. James Hastings says, "If the blood of Abel cries from the ground, shall not the blood of Christ cry from the cross for response to deathless love, and can it cry in vain?" Although we often say it was our Saviour, actually it was this heart broken prophet who first taught us to recognize God as "our Father"—the One who called and still calls his children from the bondage of sin into the glorious liberty of his redeeming love.

Invitations to Repentance
(6:1–3; 10:12–14; 14:1–9)

There are three formal calls for Israel to return to God. Each closes a section of prophetic condemnation of the people's sinful state. The second call seems to presuppose that the people had gone too far in sin to come back, for it is immediately followed by a description of coming judgment because of continued transgression.

The first invitation (6:1–3) follows the Lord's pronouncement of the nation's fate. Because Israel has walked after man rather than God three things are threatened. He will be to them as a moth and rottenness (symbolizing disintegration in national character and stability). He will be as a lion (symbolizing calamity and catastrophe). He will withdraw from their national life, leaving them to the fate of their own sin. Then the prophet calls, "Come, and let us return unto the Lord . . . and he will heal us; he hath smitten, and he will bind us up. . . . Then shall we know, if we follow on to know the Lord" (6:1-3). Included in this invitation is a reference to God's power to raise them up—the promise that on the third day Israel shall live in his sight. The messianic character of this utterance cannot be doubted. Christian era unveiled it, but the truth was present, though in embryonic form, of the resurrection of our Saviour.

Some have attempted to make the passage, 6:1-3, a "tongue in cheek" reference to a superficial repentance of Israel. This is not a necessary or even the best interpretation. This tender and beautiful appeal could be words of the people praying for restoration and forgiveness. This interpretation suits both the text and the context.

The second invitation (10:12-14) concludes the stormy section, beginning with 6:4, which pictures the iniquity and lawlessness of Israel. This discourse could easily represent the "thick night" of Israel's history when her kings were "cut off quickly like foam upon the water." Only one of Israel's last six kings died a natural death. The prophet urged the people, "Sow to yourselves in righteousness, reap in mercy; break up your fallow ground: for it is time to seek the Lord" (10:12). Hosea hardly expected national repentance, for he immediately describes calamity coming to the land as their king would be "cut off" at daybreak.

The final invitation (14:1-9) is a concluding word of promise for the whole book, as well as a call to repentance following the third major prophetic discourse (11:12 to 13:16). The final verse is an epilogue for Hosea's entire prophetic ministry.

Included in this invitation is a beautiful description of Israel as the nation will be when God's gracious forgiveness comes. Jehovah will heal their backsliding and love them freely. He will be as dew to Israel. The nation shall blossom as the lily, and her beauty shall be as the olive tree. Israel's scent shall be as the wine of Lebanon. Prosperity shall abound and the people shall be cured of idolatry. Fruit shall spring forth from the Lord's redeemed people. What a marvelous future for the wayward people if they would return to their God!

A Word to Our World

What is the message of Hosea for today? No serious student of the times, or even a casual observer, can fail to see the parallel of the prophet's day and ours. Personal and national integrity are seldom strong enough to withstand temptation. Powers and institutions divinely established to conserve the spiritual life of a people are following the path of least resistance. The norm by which greatness is evaluated is unclear. A nation's strength is measured by military power and economic strength rather than by godliness and spiritual resources. All of this was true also in Hosea's day.

The love of God, however, is strong enough to change human nature if it is surrendered to the God revealed in Jesus Christ. Love knows no length nor breadth nor depth nor height. When Fridtjof Nansen and his party were sending down their equipment to measure the depth of the Arctic Ocean, the reply came again and again, "Deeper than that." The depth of God's love likewise has never been fully comprehended. His grace is always sufficient for the repentant sinner.

NOTES

1. Sarah Williams, "Is It So, O Christ in Heaven?" *Home Book of Quotations* (New York: Dodd, Mead & Company, 1934).

2. *Best Loved Religious Poems* (New York: Fleming H. Revell Co., 1933).

3. J. B. Phillips, *Four Prophets* (New York: The Macmillan Co., 1963), p. 36.

7

Man Rebels—God Withdraws
(OBADIAH)

The prophet Obadiah and his "indignant oration" have been tossed back and forth across the centuries of Jewish history by Old Testament scholars. Several things are known about the prophet and his "Hymn of Hate," whatever the century in which he spoke.

The time was one of great calamity for Israel. The land had been attacked. Foreigners had entered the gates of Jerusalem and stripped the land naked of all its substance. The Edomites had stood on the other side and not only failed to help but actually rejoiced in Israel's tragedy. At first glance the book of Obadiah seems to have little spiritual depth and to reflect only a vindictive spirit. But closer study reveals that Obadiah made a spiritual contribution greatly needed in every generation.

S. Parkes Cadman says the book teaches that "hate silences the voice of compassion, blinds the soul's vision, corrupts the social fabric . . . and consigns . . . political systems . . . to destruction." Loyalty to one's family, one's friends, and one's nation is admirable, but not when it presumes to limit God's love, God's righteousness, or one's own moral obligation.

Considering all the evidence, the safest conclusion is that Obadiah spoke shortly after the fall of Jerusalem to Babylon in 587 B.C. No other event in Jewish history seems to provide quite the proper background for the harsh words of the prophet. He begins with a stern statement. Edom must be destroyed. There will be no respite. There is no alternative (1:1-9). Obadiah then lists the reasons why this destruction is forthcoming. Edom has been cruel and overbearing in her attitude toward her neighbor nation. She has shown no spirit of love or concern (1:10-14). The book concludes with an affirmation that in the consummation of God's purposes, Israel will be vindicated and victorious. She shall be honored and exalted by God to the consternation of her enemies.

Three words gather up the theme and set it forth for contemporary consideration: the *fault* of the Edomites, the *fury* which shall be poured out upon Edom for this cruel conduct, the *future* of Israel and Edom—especially *God's future* in the processes of history.

Fault

Wherein was Edom guilty? Why did Jehovah, through his prophet, decree such a catastrophe for the inhabitants of Seir?

She had failed to remember that Israel was her brother. For centuries this family feud had persisted. It began when the twins, Jacob and Esau, came forth struggling even from the womb. After several childhood skirmishes the boys became reconciled, but the descendants did not. Israel and Edom were perpetual enemies. Edom would not allow the Israelites to pass through her country on the way from Egypt to the Promised Land, although Moses gave them every assurance that they would not harm the land in any way nor drink any of the water from the wells (Num. 20:17). This wicked refusal showed the true attitude of Edom. She rejoiced in every hardship that Israel was called upon to endure.

Edom was not a people who worshiped idols. The Philistines had Dagon, the Phoenicians had Baal and Ashtaroth, the Ammonites had Molech, the Moabites had Chemosh, but the Edomites had no national deity to whom they gave allegiance and loyalty. Edom represents the man of worldly wisdom and sophistication who needs no strength but his own and is thoroughly liberated from the need of spiritual guidance and "religious crutches." This spirit began with Esau who was the self-sufficient sophisticate in contrast to Jacob who, in spite of his faults, was a more deeply religious man.

The people of Edom were a proud people. Pride always accompanies an attitude which feels no need of the spiritual. Edom was filled with pride in her economic independence. Recent archaeological discoveries reveal that Edom carried on extensive trade with nearby countries and distant lands. From Elath, at the head of the Gulf of Aqaba, Edom's ships sailed as far as India and returned with argosies of freight. Trade routes spread across Palestine and went northward to Damascus. Great copper mines and smelting furnaces brought wealth and commercial expansion. Edom was interested, not in culture nor ideals, but in things. John Paterson in *The Goodly Fellowship of the Prophets* says, "Edom represents the proud, haughty spirit that trusts itself, and, as such, it was radically opposed to the religious mood and temper of Israel. At the center of Israel's life was . . . the vital thought of a sovereign God; at the center of Edom's life was a market place."

Edom's pride became arrogance. A major reason for this attitude was the impregnable position of her fortresses. When the country was attacked, the people withdrew to the interior of the land which was inaccessible except by passage through the rocky honeycombs. For instance, one could enter Petra, the capital, only by passing through a narrow gorge more than a mile long. Isolated from the world and insulated against invasion, the arrogant Edomites could scorn every effort to displace them. They carried on raiding expeditions against caravans of merchantmen, then fled to safety in the rocky clefts. This smug satisfaction caused Obadiah to declare, "You who live in the clefts of the rock, whose dwelling is high, who say in your heart, 'Who will bring me down to the ground?'" (v. 3, RSV).

Gazing on Edom's conduct in the day of Israel's calamity Obadiah was shocked by this shameful neutrality as the people of God were assailed and their land devastated. Obadiah was stirred to righteous indignation and hot anger because, in the day of Israel's direst need, Edom was content to be a mere onlooker in the drama. Obadiah saw in the situation more than a battle between two enemies. Israel represented God's revelation of light, morality, and religious principle. Babylon represented pagan militarism, godless and unrighteous. Edom preferred to remain neutral because she was unwilling to jeopardize her security or suffer inconvenience to help sustain a people seeking to uphold principles of law and morality.

As usual indifference led to direct injury. At first, Edom merely stood aloof on the other side the day that strangers carried away Israel's substance and foreigners entered into the gates and cast lots upon Jerusalem (v. 11, RSV.) Soon however, Edom was rejoicing over Jerusalem's destruction and speaking proudly in the day of Judah's distress (v. 12). Later, Edom laid hands on their substance (v. 13) then stood at the place of retreat cutting off those who sought escape.

Obadiah suggests that the Edomites even delivered to the enemy those who remained (v. 14).

It is a terrible thing to be neutral in a time when one is needed on the battlefield! Henry of Navarré reportedly said to a general under his command, "Go hang yourself brave Crillon. There was a battle fought and you were not there." John Ker says, "When truth is in danger, the conduct of many is to wash their hands in Pilate's basin of weak neutrality, but they only soil the water and do not cleanse their hands."

Fury

Many Old Testament prophets speak of a general judgment in which all nations will be involved. This will be the day of the Lord, the day when God's purposes will be realized. Upon the enemies of Israel God will pour out his wrath, and these enemies will be more completely subjected than ever before in Israel's history. No matter how hopeless the situation or how completely God's enemies seemed to gain the victory, the prophet always saw the defeat of Israel's enemies and the cup of fury poured out upon the nations who defied God's moral law.

Edom will not escape God's fury! When the eagle builds his nest, he puts it in a place virtually inaccessible to man. The Edomites might have been called a race of eagles. Obadiah warned, however, that "though thou exalt thyself as the eagle, and though thou set thy nest among the stars, thence will I bring thee down, saith the Lord" (v. 4).

This proud spirit was responsible for Edom's attitude toward Israel. Her comfortable complacency, rooted in pride, made her indifferent to Israel's calamity. Her neutrality was rooted in self-sufficiency which produced her haughty spirit.

No wonder pride is listed as first of the deadly sins. Lance Webb says, "It is pride which curses and destroys so many of us and adds to the destruction of our world," and negatively paraphrases the first Beatitude, "Wretched are the proud in spirit for they shall never enter the kingdom of heaven."

Pride must be punished! Billy Graham says that pride, "because it trusts in one's own virtue rather than the grace of God, is earmarked for God's judgment." The author of Job shared Obadiah's attitude concerning the punishment of pride. "Though his height mount up to the heavens, and his head reach to the clouds, he will perish for ever like his own dung; those who have seen him will say, 'Where is he?' " (20:6–7, RSV).

Not only pride shall come under the condemnation of God. The nauseating neutrality of Edom which retreated into inaction was equally repulsive to God. Many years before, Deborah and Barak, singing a victory chant after the defeat of Sisera, expressed utter dissatisfaction with neutrality in a time when assistance was needed: "Curse Meroz, says the angel of the Lord, curse bitterly its inhabitants, because they came not to the help of the Lord, to the help of the Lord against the mighty" (Judg. 5:23, RSV).

Long before Paul warned the worldly-wise inhabitants of Corinth that mere human wisdom was foolishness and God would destroy the wisdom of the wise and bring to nothing the understanding of the prudent (1 Cor. 1:19), Obadiah warned the sophisticates of Edom that God's punitive hand would be upon them. "Will I not on that day, says the Lord, destroy the wise men out of Edom, and understanding out of Mount Esau?" (v. 8, RSV). Even more severely he continued, "Your mighty men shall be dismayed, O Teman, so that every man from Mount Esau will be cut off by slaughter" (v. 9,

RSV). Obadiah was no solitary, vindictive spirit different
from the other canonical prophets. Isaiah with equal harshness
condemned pride. He warned the king of Babylon, "The worm
is spread under thee, and worms cover thee. . . . "Thou saidst
in thy heart, I will ascend into heaven, I will exalt my throne
above the stars of God; . . . I will ascend above the heights
of the clouds; I will make myself like the Most High. Yet
thou shalt be brought down . . . to the uttermost parts of
the pit" (14:11–15, ASV).

When the final judgment comes, the profane person who
has shown no concern for God cannot expect mercy from the
God he has never known. Edom's perspective had been
twisted. Cloistered safely from other nations and dwelling
where the broken country fell away for miles and miles into
the hot distance of piled up purple hills, Edom's sense of
rightness had endured decay. She had looked down from the
hills and sneered at humanity. On her puckered tablecloth
of pale brown, man, God's greatest masterpiece, appeared
as a mere ant. Van Zeller, a Catholic scholar, says, "The eagle
Edom sat upon the landscape as if she had hatched it." Such
an attitude could not go unnoticed or unpunished.

Edom must fall! As Cain was forced to become a fugitive
and vagabond because he failed his brother, so was proud
Edom brought low and left in a barren land among sharp
rocks. Jeremiah saw the coming judgment and Edom's em-
barrassment as his secret places were uncovered and he was
unable to hide himself. According to Jeremiah, Bozrah, one
of Edom's chief cities, "shall become an astonishment, a re-
proach, a waste, and a curse; . . . every one that passeth by
it shall be astonished, and shall hiss at all the plagues thereof
(Jer. 49:13–17, ASV).

Edom would feel God's avenging hand. The nation could

not escape the moral law of the universe nor the punitive action of Jehovah. Obadiah says emphatically that "the day of the Lord is near upon all the nations. As you have done, it shall be done to you, your deeds shall return on your own head" (v. 15, RSV).

Future

Obadiah's most meaningful contribution is not his sharp words of condemnation against Edom because of her arrogance and despicable attitude toward Israel. Great preaching never merely threatens judgment because of repeated transgressions. To pronounce God's severity toward sin is necessary, but to proclaim the glory of God's companionship is inspiring.

Obadiah saw the future! He saw God's purposes being worked out in the historical processes. Part of this future was the elimination of Edom as a factor in history, and it came true as Obadiah declared. All the historical records are not available, and complete facts as to the time when the Edomites were dislodged from their rocky, purple-mountained stronghold are not known. But, Jeremiah predicted that Babylon would lead Edom away captive. Assuming that this happened, the Edomites did not have long to digest Obadiah's warnings before they were fulfilled. When the Jews returned from Babylonian exile in 536 B.C., they found the Edomites inhabiting the Negeb, south of Judah, and the mountain of Judah as far north as Hebron. Obadiah's words had become a reality.

What about Judah? When Obadiah spoke, the people were devastated. The day of her calamity was upon her. Was there any future for this handful of captives whose city had been razed and whose Temple had been burned? Had the hope for Judah's future as God's people gone up in the flame and smoke that consumed the Temple, and did it now lie in ashes even as the great house of God?

Obadiah saw the purpose of God's mighty acts in history. No matter how dark the outlook, the divine plan would emerge victorious. Mount Zion once more would become holy through the remnant that would return. God's people would recover their possessions. Deliverers would come to Mount Zion to be judges. The kingdom would be the Lord's. This is the great message of Obadiah.

It is never easy to evaluate properly contemporary events or movements. What seems all important to one generation may become very insignificant when tested by time. Every generation needs men who can see beyond the temporal and perceive the eternal. John Ruskin was right when he said that for every ten men who can talk there is only one who can think, and for every ten men who can think there is only one who can see. Obadiah saw beyond Judah's present disaster to the glory of God's plan for her. Only a few in each generation are men of vision. The spiritual voice within to which one yields, not the physical environment without, makes the difference. When Chief Justice Marshall visited the mountains of Virginia he exclaimed, "No wonder Patrick Henry was an orator." An old farmer replied, "Young man, those mountains have been there ever since, but we've never had another Patrick Henry." A contemporary Christian prays, "God grant us the wisdom to see—the angel in the marble, the oak in the acorn, the blossom in the bud, the building in the barn, the dawn in the darkness, the gold in the boulder, the future in the present and God in everything."

The words of Obadiah have unquestioned relevance for today's world. Entrenched evil must be overthrown. Pride, though it mount up as eagles, must be brought down. Neutrality concerning the great moral struggles for righteousness and justice is condemned. Jesus expressed the theme of Obadiah, "He that is not with me is against me; and he that gathereth not with me scattereth abroad" (Matt. 12:30). To stand idly by when God's cause needs support is equivalent to aiding the forces of unrighteousness.

> I never cut my neighbor's throat,
> My neighbor's gold I never stole;
> I never spoiled his house or land,
> But God have mercy on my soul!
>
> For I am haunted night and day,
> By all the deeds I have not done;
> O unattempted loveliness!
> O costly valor never won! [1]

Obadiah's message is more than a "Hymn of Hate." The forces of evil will not have the last word. The kingdom belongs to God. He remains King of kings and Lord of lords. In every area of life he should reign supreme!

NOTES

1. Marguerite Wilkins, "Guilty," *A Thousand Quotable Poems* (Chicago: Willett Clark & Company, 1937) p. 119.

8

God's Love and His Law
(MALACHI)

"Eternal vigilance is the price of liberty." Perennial prophetic preaching is essential to a continuity of morality among the people of any nation. God never leaves himself without a witness. James Stewart says that when any generation "has been robbed of its familiar gods of material security, progress, human self-sufficiency . . . by the marauding forces of agnosticism, trouble and despair, then strikes God's hour." Such a time had come for Judah. Haggai and Zechariah had led the people to build the Temple, but now a great retrogression was happening in the spiritual life of the nation. There was a need for a man of God to declare the divine counsel without compromise. Such a man was available! He was the last of the Old Testament prophets, but by no means was he the least!

There is a paucity of information concerning all the Minor Prophets. In the case of Malachi, the uncertainty extends even to his name. Some scholars believe that the word should be translated "my messenger," and that the book is an anonymous work by a contemporary of Ezra and Nehemiah. However, sufficient scholars doubt this belief to make the matter an open question. The average Bible student probably is more interested in an analysis of the message than the name.

The style of Malachi is different from any other prophet. He follows Socrates' method of question and answer with a slight variation. A statement of truth is followed by the people's objection to this truth. His reply restates and strengthens the original proposition. This style became popular in Judaism among the rabbis. Malachi has been called "the Hebrew Socrates" and was the "forerunner of Scholastic Rabbinism."

When Malachi lived, the golden age of prophecy had waned, but his insights equalled and, in some cases, exceeded anything to be found in prophetic literature. Some scholars do not believe that certain concepts in this postexilic period could have come from Malachi. The concept of the universalism of God's kingdom, the high and holy view of marriage, the teaching that divine love is holy love rooted in God's majesty and the standard of conduct which the prophet demanded in God's name from the people—all of these put Malachi on the same lofty plane as Amos, Micah, or even Isaiah. There is nothing inferior or second-rate about this final Old Testament spokesman for God. If the prophetic movement was on the decline, here is a glorious exception to the trend. Malachi stood far above any man of his day. He compares favorably with any prophet of any period.

A brief review of the times in which the prophet lived will increase appreciation for the man and his message. A study of the book will mean much more when the historical background is known. It is not easy to find an analytical outline for Malachi's prophecies. Three great themes pervade the message. The relevance of Malachi's prophecy to contemporary life will be more easily seen by an analysis of these themes. The first is closely related to the historical background.

Difficulties and Discouragements

The bitter frustrations of the postexilic age left deep scars upon the soul of Israel. The returning captives arrived at Jerusalem with tremendous enthusiasm. They aspired to re-establish the glorious days of Israel comparable to the golden age of David's reign. They were certain that the promises of the preexilic and exilic prophets would come to pass with amazing and literal accuracy in their day. The land would produce a miraculous abundance, and all nations would serve them.

Every dreamer must eventually come face to face with reality. The returning exiles found life difficult. Actually, only a few of the great number in Babylon decided to come back to their homeland. The new Jewish settlement was only a tiny colony in the great Persian Empire. The land was stony and unproductive. When they attempted to build, they met with ridicule and forceful opposition from people in the near-by land. Frustration and discouragement set in quickly.

Ezra and Nehemiah were two strong individuals who played an important part in the history of this period. The facts about the relationship of these men and their work are not too difficult to ascertain. When the Temple was completed in 516 B.C., there was a great dedication. The Passover was observed, and for a period of time there was a spiritual surge among the people. But in a short time the new wore off and the "honeymoon period" was over. In 458 B.C., Ezra, a Jewish scribe, led another group from Babylon to Jerusalem. He came to teach the law to the returned Israelites. He found a disappointing situation. The people had wandered far from proper observance of the Mosaic law. They had become care-less about their tithes and offerings. They had been unfaithful to their marriage vows. Many had forsaken the "wife of their youth" to marry foreign women. A general religious indifference had settled over the land. Even the spiritual leaders had neglected their responsibility. A skepticism toward godly matters in general had developed among the people. There was need for a great religious revival. Under the ministry of Ezra, the people made a fresh start and much good was affected.

The story of Nehemiah is one of the most thrilling in Old Testament history. Leaving a place of personal prestige in the king's service, this dedicated layman, at virtually his own expense, journeyed to Jerusalem and led the people to rebuild a great wall around the city to replace the one which had been destroyed. In spite of much opposition, the task was completed in only fifty-two days! The date of this campaign was about 444 B.C.

At the conclusion of this building activity, Ezra returned to conduct another teaching program. Conditions were similar to those earlier. The people had either continued, or begun again, to ignore the teachings of God with reference to moral responsibility. Skepticism and cynicism had set in, and a general feeling of apathy and unconcern had developed. More than mere teaching was needed. A great prophetic voice was needed to shout with courage and conviction the demands of a holy God. Such a person was Malachi. The exact date of his ministry is unknown, but it was during this period of discouragement and moral retrogression.

Accusations and Answers

Perhaps the greatest problem of the people in this post-exilic society was unawareness that they had a problem. Each time the prophet brought an accusation they had an answer.

Thomas Carlyle said, "The greatest of faults is to be conscious of none." This is an exact description of the inhabitants of Jerusalem in the mid-fifth century before Christ.

One of the best approaches to the first three chapters of Malachi is to analyze the seven charges which the prophet made against the people.

1. I have loved you, saith the Lord.
   Yet ye say, Wherein hast thou loved us? (1:2)
2. O priests, that despise my name.
   And ye say, Wherein have we despised thy name? (1:6)
3. Ye offer polluted bread upon mine altar;
   And ye say, Wherein have we polluted thee? (1:7)
4. Ye have wearied the Lord with your words.
   Yet ye say, Wherein have we wearied him? (2:17)
5. Return unto me, and I will return unto you, saith the Lord of hosts.
   But ye said, Wherein shall we return? (3:7)
6. Will a man rob God? Yet ye have robbed me.
   But ye say, Wherein have we robbed thee? (3:8)
7. Your words have been stout against me, saith the Lord.
   Yet ye say, What have we spoken so much against thee? (3:13)

These replies represent the sophisticated self-righteousness of one who imagines he has "arrived" in moral behavior. They are the words of a people who believe that they have intellectual acumen and consequently play at religion, fancying themselves superior to anyone, even God himself. Certainly they did not intend to listen to a prophet. "He is but a man! How dare he condemn us! He doesn't even fit in our circle! His very presence is an affront to our prestige and offensive to our group!" Ernst Sellin observes that this period was one where the prophet must resort to the argumentative method. The people were no longer patient with preaching. They resented it with all their sophisticated and sin-sick souls.

The first accusation reveals that, although Malachi could speak forcefully of God's wrath, he believed love was the master key which opened all doors. His book begins with a charge that the people had been recipients of God's gracious blessings and had failed to realize that every good thing received came from their God. Theodore Parker calls gratitude "a touch of beauty added to the countenance giving an angelic loveliness to character," while Joseph Joubert speaks of gratitude as "the memory of the heart."

When the people asked for proof of God's love, he showed them the difference in Jacob's descendants and those of Esau. Both nations had their problems, but as George L. Robinson reminds us, there was a great difference: "Jacob was *disciplined* only—being brought from exile; Whereas Esau was *punished*—being left in captivity."

To deny God's love is to say he is the very opposite of what he claims. Perhaps nothing breaks the heart of parents more than a child's suspicion of their motives. God's moral law is not based on a capricious desire to dominate but to assure the best for his children.

The prophet next accuses the people of despising Jehovah's name. Throughout the Old Testament the *name* of a person is often significant. The character is usually inseparable from the name. Jehovah is more accurately rendered Yahweh. It is the imperfect form of the verb "to be" and signifies the eternal and unchanging nature of God. For the people to give less than their best in his service is to "despise his name." Many contemporary scholars see a new meaning in the Third Commandment of the Decalogue. To take God's name in vain is to bear his name without matching his character. The disciples were called Christians because their character reminded the people of the person whom they professed. Malachi ac-

cused the religious leaders of dishonoring God by rendering
shabby and second-rate service in his name.

The third accusation was quickly answered by the con-
tentious people. They denied that they were offering polluted
bread. The prophet challenged them to dare offer the same
loyalty to their governor that they offered to their God. Malachi declared that it would be better to close the doors of
God's house and forget the whole thing than to continue such
halfhearted support of God's cause. He shouted, "Oh, that
there were one among you who would shut the doors, that
you might not kindle fire upon my altar in vain! I have no
pleasure in you, says the Lord of hosts, and I will not accept
an offering from your hand" (1:10, RSV).

Malachi spoke harsh words to the people for bringing
blemished offerings to God, but he had a sterner rebuke for
the priests. They should have held high the standards of law
and morality. But they "have turned aside from the way . . .
have caused many to stumble . . . have corrupted the covenant of Levi" (2:8, RSV). Therefore, God assigned to them
a place of contempt.

Marriage vows have always been important. The men of
Judah had left the wives of their youth and gone after
foreign women. Malachi reminded the men that their wedded
wives were their companions, and that God intended for men
to have only one wife in order that they might produce godly
families. Malachi considered the worst result of divorce to be
its effect on the children. The prophet left no question as to
God's attitude, "I hate divorce, says the Lord" (2:16, RSV).

The prophet's fourth charge was that the people doubted
either God's integrity or his judgment, or both. When Malachi
accused the people of wearying the Lord with words, they
demanded proof. He replied, "You do it when by your actions
you say, Every one who does evil is good in the sight of the

Lord, and He delights in them. Or by *asking*, Where is the God of justice?" (2:17, Amplified Old Testament).

When trials come and sorrows accumulate, strong faith is difficult to maintain. Men ask why God permits the wicked to live and enjoy life while obedient servants suffer adversity and shame. Laetsch reminds us that this is not the language of faith. It is that of self-centeredness, unbelief and presumptuous pride. He says, "Puny man . . . criticising the eternal Jehovah, his Creator and Redeemer, simply because he cannot comprehend Him whose ways are past finding out. . . . Unbelief is a damnable sin, whether found in manifestly wicked scoffers or in the heart of professed believers." The people had wearied the Lord with their words of complaint and criticism. They were on the verge of being rejected. Yet there was hope if they would return.

Accusations number five and six are linked together. The prophet sent out a clarion call for repentance, "Return unto me, and I will return unto you" (3:7). The people asked what the prophet meant by such a statement. In what area of life did they need to mend their ways? He accused them of robbery. They had failed to bring their tithes into God's storehouse. God's work was suffering because the people failed to provide the material resources necessary to carry on this work.

Financial support for God's program is an ever-present problem. If Christian people would practice stewardship— even the minimum of a tithe—a great world mission endeavor could be projected. Without debating the obligation of the Christian to fulfil the legalistic requirements of the Old Testament, certainly no Christian should give less under grace than the Jew was required to give under the Law. An old truism says, "You can give without loving, but you cannot love without giving." One gauge of a man's dedication is whether he

handles his money or his money handles him. Clifton Allen
(if I remember rightly) once said:

Money measures men—their capacity and their consecration. In
some instances money masters men. They become its slaves. In
many instances money multiplies men. Through the ministry of the
money he earns and gives, a Christian labors on every continent,
preaches in a thousand pulpits, teaches and trains tomorrow's
leaders.

According to Malachi, failure to support God's work is to
rob God. Raymond Calkins, in *The Modern Message of the
Minor Prophets* says, "The loose way in which many members
bear their plain obligations to the church they have vowed to
support is a scandal. . . . It is said that nowadays the work
and support of a church is borne by one-third of its congre-
gation; another third looks on; and the remaining third does
not know what it is all about." We rob ourselves of joy and
happiness when we fail to support God's work with our
money. Malachi put it stronger. He declared that Israel was
an ungrateful nation of robbers. They had defrauded God of
his due. Are not church members who refuse to bring God's
money into the storehouse also robbers in his sight?

A twofold promise is made to the people if they will accept God's challenge to be faithful in their giving. God will
pour out a blessing. Many faithful stewards testify that the
blessing is not always necessarily a material one. God can
bless a life or a home many ways other than to increase
wealth or possessions. God promised to vindicate Judah in
the presence of her enemies. This was an important promise
to a group literally "squeezed in" by those who were antag-
onistic to their way of life and their God. Continued crop
failures were interpreted by Judah's enemies as a sign of God's
displeasure with the people. If the people would be faithful

in giving their money, God would remove this stigma, and the nation would become a delight in the eyes of themselves and others.

The final accusation was parallel to the fourth. This one records that the people spoke "stout" words against the Lord rather than merely wearying him with words. Their language was harsh and offensive concerning the Lord and his work. They resented the prophet's charge, insisting they had not spoken against God. But the prophet quickly reminded them of their own words, "It is useless to serve God; . . . what profit is it if we keep His ordinances?" (3:14, Amplified Old Testament).

These people had become bitter and cynical—"idealism gone sour in the face of frustration." This was the condition of the Jews in postexilic days. They had expected great things but wanted them too quickly. When they did not happen immediately, the people had become impatient, then critical of God.

Malachi's message is one of "prophecy within the law" or "All's love, yet all's law." God loved his people. He had chosen them, blessed them, and when necessary, disciplined them. Law is basic to any society. Some govern the very universe itself. A people cannot ignore the basic laws of humanity in the belief that God is love. Law cannot be violated with impunity. The laws of God are for us if we permit, against us if we insist. Even God's love is grounded in law.

Problems and Promises

When difficulties arise, some people magnify the problems, others magnify the promises of God. Malachi knew Judah's serious problems as a nation, but he was convinced of God's power to deal with any contingency.

Early in his prophecy, Malachi insisted the day would come when the Lord's name would be great throughout all nations. He declared, "From the rising of the sun even unto the going down of the same my name shall be great among the Gentiles; and in every place incense shall be offered unto my name, and a pure offering: for my name shall be great . . . saith the Lord of hosts" (1:11). Of course, the present plight of the Jews made such a statement ludicrous. How could this feeble group ever impress the world with the quality of their religious faith or the worth of their God? The situation seemed hopeless and cynics asked, "Where is the god of justice?" (2:17, RSV).

The prophet had an answer—God's answer. God will send his messenger. He will prepare the way, and the Lord will suddenly come to his temple (3:1). John the Baptist was the messenger who prepared the way. Jesus Christ was the "messenger of the covenant."

This sounds like a day of victory for Israel and a time of triumph over her foes. But Malachi was addressing Jews when he said "Who can endure the day of his coming?" (3:2, RSV). If the people were expecting a confirmation of their conduct, they were to be disappointed. The messenger was coming to execute a terrible judgment upon them. Their moral and spiritual failures made it impossible for the people to stand in the pure light of God's holiness. He would be a refiner's fire. All the impure ingredients mixed with the precious metal would be burned. He would be like a fuller's soap which eats deep into the tissues.

The purpose of the refiner and the fuller is not to destroy but to purify and make perfect through cleansing. Every redeemed person knows the value of daily discipline that assures victory in the battle between flesh and spirit. Theodore

Laetsch in *The Minor Prophets* says, "This is necessary, since
the believer's flesh ceaselessly battles against the new spiritual
life. Daily the Refiner purges away the dross and takes away
all tin. No matter how highly polished, it is worthless dross,
and as such is removed by the Purifier, the Searcher of hearts.
Though painful, it is a necessary, a blessed work, for which
the believer will in time and eternity thank his Refiner."

The prophet concludes with a section concerning God's
activity in the days to come. One of the most beautiful promises in the Scriptures follows a judgment upon evildoers. All
the proud and the workers of wickedness shall be stubble.
They shall be burned so thoroughly that neither branch nor
root shall remain. The fierce flames crackle for a moment as
they consume the ungodly, leaving only white ashes. A different future for God's people is prophesied. The Messiah is
described as the Sun of righteousness; he shall come with
healing in his wings. The bruised and faithful people would
react with gladness to such a vision. The rays of the rising sun
would bring fresh hope for the discouraged remnant. The
dawn of a new day always brings hope to weary souls. The
poet Walter Malone says,

> Weep not for precious chances passed away,
> Wail not for golden ages on the wane
> Each night I burn the records of the day
> At sunrise every soul is born again.[1]

The Sun of righteousness is also the divine physician for sin-
sick souls. The gospel is healing for humanity's hurt, peace for
troubled minds, comfort for sorrowing hearts, and forgiveness
for guilty sinners. Jesus is the fulfilment of this gracious promise. Alexander Maclaren points out that in admiration for the

beautiful poetry one should not forget the truth in God's oracle. Each person must settle for himself "whether that day shall be a furnace to destroy or a sun to cheer and enlighten."

The last three verses of Malachi's work are a proper conclusion for the entire prophetical section of the Old Testament. The prophets were not opponents of the Law or destroyers of legal codes or priestly functions. They were interpreters of the Law seeking to reinforce its teaching, give it spirit, and make it relevant to life. No society can exist without law or become moral without more than law. The moral dynamic necessary for obedience is present only when love motivates. Malachi enjoined the people to "remember ye the law of Moses" (4:4).

Before the coming of the great day of the Lord, God will send Elijah to relate the people properly to one another. There will be one last great effort to convert the people before judgment comes. New Testament Christians saw in John the Baptist the fulfilment of this prediction. S. L. Edgar says that John's preaching was directed "against those who infringed, not just the ceremonial, but the moral and spiritual demands of God. . . . By demanding repentance he was preparing for the ministry of Jesus Christ."

Malachi did not set priest and law against prophet and prophecy. The choice was not between law or prophecy or between law and love. In any generation—the fifth century before Christ in Judah or the twentieth century after him in America—each must be present to reinforce the other! Browning was incontestably correct, "All's love, yet all's law!"

NOTES

1. Walter Malone, "Opportunity." Used by permission of the Malone family.

9

A Man for the Time
(HAGGAI)

In 587 B.C. the Temple in Jerusalem was burned. With few exceptions, the people who remained from the previous deportations (605 and 597 B.C.), were carried captive to Babylon. For the next half century the Jews remained in this foreign country. Although separated from their homeland, they did not fare too badly. A limited amount of freedom was given to them. They were permitted to build their houses, cultivate their gardens, and worship God according to their wishes. During this period the synagogue came into being and a great respect for the Law arose. Idolatry was purged from Jewish life, and an intense longing developed for the Messiah.

In 539 B.C. Cyrus the Great conquered Babylon. This youthful king was quite different from most men of war. He encouraged religious freedom among his captive peoples. One of his first official acts in Babylon was to issue a decree permitting the Jewish population to return to their homeland.

Eagerly, the Jews began their homeward trek. However their joyful anticipation gave way to bitter disappointment when they saw the Holy City. Nothing was left of Jerusalem's glory which had been praised in Israel's jubilant hymns of the Exile. The walls were heaps of trash and refuse. The Temple was a pile of charred and blackened stones. The streets were overgrown with weeds.

After the first emptiness of heart was passed, they went to work. The altar was set on its old site. Sacrifices were offered as in preexilic days. They next began to rebuild the Temple. Carpenters, masons, and other workmen were hired for the task. Cedar trees were brought from Tyre and Sidon. In the second year after their return, the foundation was completed. A great service of praise was held, but emotions were mingled. Some shouted for joy because the foundation was laid; others wept as they remembered the glory and adornment of the former Temple and saw how inferior this new house of worship was destined to be. H. I. Hester says, "The general plan and size were the same as Solomon's; the chief difference was in the quality. None of the costly and ornate furnishings and refinements of the former Temple could be had for this structure."

Soon after the foundation was laid, a major problem arose. People living in the nearby land asked for the privilege of helping to rebuild the Temple. They insisted that they worshiped the same God and traced their heritage back to the Northern Kingdom. Actually, these people were a mixed race which had been started by the Assyrians when they captured Israel in 722 B.C. When the majority of the population was deported to Assyria, the people who remained intermarried with captives from other lands who were sent in by Assyria. A half-breed race had developed from these marriages. These were the Samaritans. This was the group who wanted to help in building the Temple.

The problem involved is an oft-repeated story in every age.

It is one of accepting material assistance from people who are not in full sympathy with spiritual objectives. Zerubbabel and Jeshua recognized the problems involved in receiving help from these Samaritans. The refusal was quite definite. "You have nothing to do with us in building a house to our God; but we alone will build" (Ezra 4:3, RSV).

Upon being refused, the Samaritans showed their true spirit. If they could not have a part, they would destroy the work. They "weakened the hands of the people of Judah, and troubled them in building, and hired counsellors against them, to frustrate their purpose" (Ezra 4:4–5). Later, they wrote to Artaxerxes, a successor to Cyrus, urging that he use force to cause the work to cease. The building program was stopped by opposition! How contemporary this sounds!

For approximately fifteen years nothing was done. The people worshiped amid the ruins and rubbish of an unfinished building. In spite of bad seasons, the people built their houses and provided for their comfort. Some, perhaps many, further beautified their homes, while the Lord's house still remained in a crude and incomplete state.

Then the prophet Haggai appeared on the scene. He had one mission and one message. The broken spirit of the people must be reanimated. They must be roused from their lethargy and unconcern. They must be motivated to turn from their selfish preoccupation with secular interests and dedicate their energies afresh to building God's house.

Little is known about Haggai personally. The Hebrew name means "festal" or "festive." This may indicate he was born on a feast day. Most scholars think he was advanced in years. John Paterson, however, contends that "The qualities which he reveals are not usually found in old men."

Whether young or old, Haggai had the ability to arouse

enthusiasm and inspire the people. His fervent spirit was contagious. He was joined two months later by a younger contemporary, Zechariah, whose book of prophecies follow immediately in the Old Testament canon.

Both men made contributions. Haggai was the more practical. This single minded, militantly national prophet had a remarkable genius for organization and expertly got things done—"a steam engine in trousers."

Haggai's messages are clear and concise. The four prophecies contain a total of thirty-eight verses, and in all probability, a concise summary of the prophet's oracles rather than a complete record of all words spoken. Another unique feature is that all four discourses are precisely dated. Each message has a distinct theme, yet the four are interrelated. They were timely for Judah and are relevant for today.

Exhortation (1:1-15)

The true prophet in any generation possesses insight for the needs of the hour. With keen discernment Haggai knew that, above all other things, Judah's Temple must be rebuilt if her faith was to survive.

To be sure, there must have been free thinkers or self-styled intellectuals who disagreed with this philosophy. Had not Judah learned in Babylon that the visible institution was not essential to a perpetuation of the religious principle? These sophisticated intellectuals who live in an isolated and rarefied atmosphere of spiritual quality, like the poor, are always present. They have liberated themselves from the shackles of ecclesiasticism and have no need of external crutches. The contemporary devotee of this philosophy is not ashamed of his failure to support the institutional church, but on the contrary, is proud of his detachment. He imagines he has gone beyond to a higher concept. Elton Trueblood says of such a person, "He may be tolerant of his few neighbors who still support and cherish what seems to him an outgrown institution, but he certainly is not tempted to follow their quaint example."

Haggai was not brainwashed by such thinking. He perceived the matter aright. He knew that this supposed emancipation from forms and ceremonies sounded very noble, but most people require religion that is embodied in practical and tangible goals. He knew that the nation could not prosper without a visible institution. This visible institution would become a rallying point for the social and religious life of the people.

History has vindicated the judgment of Haggai. In order to build Christian influence it is necessary to build the institutions of Christianity. Private and individual religion is necessary and important, but Christianity has never existed permanently without expressing itself in institutional forms. Evelyn Underhill in *The Life of the Spirit and the Life of Today* says, "It is a truism that religious institutions tend to degenerate, to become mechanical, to tyrannize, but . . . is it not equally a truism that without the stabilizing and preservative influence of religious institutions, the religion of pure spirit would tend to evaporate . . . or at least would fail to condense in forms of practical spiritual energy?" A visible church is as necessary for the preservation of Christianity as a dynamic force in our day as the Temple was for the perpetuation of God's purpose in the days of Haggai. "If we believe that this world needs nothing so much as the renovating influence of religion we must renew our loyalty to the visible church and help to rebuild the institutions of religion on which its permanence and effectiveness depend" (Raymond

Calkins). Loyalty does not necessarily mean a denial of the visible church's limitations and imperfections. But greater problems are involved when people minimize loyalty to the local church.

As Haggai preached, he anticipated the excuses of the people. Those who insisted that it was not the time to build were reprimanded: "Is it a time for you yourselves to dwell in your paneled houses, while this house lies in ruins?" (v. 4, RSV). The prophet boldly connected their economic setbacks with God's displeasure in their refusal to build the house of the Lord. "You have looked for much, and, lo, it came to little; and when you brought it home, I blew it away. Why? says the Lord of hosts. Because of my house that lies in ruins, while you busy yourselves each with his own house" (v. 9, RSV).

The preaching of Haggai was effective. The people realized that they had preferred personal comfort and expensive conveniences to completing God's house. The leaders were stirred up by the Spirit of God and led the people to resume building. According to the record (v. 1), Haggai began preaching on the first day of the sixth month of Darius' second year. The last verse in chapter 1 records that the people began the work on the twenty-fourth day of the sixth month. What powerful preaching! In twenty-three days Haggai rebuked their indifference, filled them with enthusiasm, and created a spirit of willingness. Actual operations began, and the building program was once more on its way!

Encouragement (2:1-9)

The task of the prophet is twofold. He is to comfort the afflicted and afflict the comfortable. Sometimes God's people need to be rebuked for their complacency and unconcern.

Other times they need comfort and encouragement. A wise prophet knows which the people need at a given time.

After about three and one-half weeks of building, the people became discouraged. They realized that the Temple they were building would fall far short of the glory of the first Temple. Perhaps some critical comparisons were made.

This attitude is a normal one. When the first enthusiasm for a difficult task declines, obstacles encountered grow larger. There were only a few people. Building materials were costly. Some had to be brought from a long distance. Judah had no allies such as Solomon had to aid with the work. There were no resources to draw on, and soon all ready funds were exhausted. What could be done? Some suggested that they quit work and give up the project entirely. They thought, If we can't build something as beautiful as Solomon built, why bother at all?

Haggai was a realist. He admitted immediately that if the two Temples were judged by outward standards, the one under construction would be disappointing. However, the prophet insisted that the glory of the second Temple would be greater than that of the first. God had more wonderful things for the future. The past had brought ruin and scattering, but better days were ahead because God's presence with them was assured. Haggai declared, "Be strong . . . for I am with you, saith the Lord of hosts" (v. 4). God's covenant made at the time of the Exodus was still in effect. There was no need to fear or to be discouraged.

The next words of Haggai (vv. 6–7) are probably the greatest in his prophecy. He said that God was about to act in history for a great purpose. The earth and the kingdoms of it were about to be shaken. A cataclysmic upheaval was about to take place among the nations, and when the tumult had

subsided God would be honored and his house glorified. Within these words of assurance was a great promise, "The desire
of all nations shall come" (v. 7).

As to the meaning of this passage, two questions may be
raised. Was Haggai mistaken in expecting an immediate
"shaking of the nations" that would usher in the glory of the
Messiah and his kingdom? He was no more in error in expecting a speedy fulfilment of God's promise than were the
New Testament writers who looked for an imminent coming
of Jesus in their day. Vital faith always looks expectantly
for God's power to be made manifest and his work to prosper
in the immediate future or the present moment. A living
faith produces this attitude.

The other question concerns the phrase "desire of all nations." In these Hebrew words a singular noun appears with
a plural verb. The King James word "desire" is the most
natural translation of the Hebrew word "hamdath." The
problem is the plural verb which is translated "shall come."
Does this govern the noun and give it a plural force,
"desirable things," and thus minimize its messianic thrust?
Was Haggai merely declaring that the wealth of the heathen
nations would pour into the earthly sanctuary of the Jews, or
was he referring to the coming of a personal Messiah?

The answer to this question lies in the concept and understanding of messianic prophecy. Quite often, the prophet
made statements that had an immediate application for the
local situation but whose ultimate fulfilment had far greater
depth and meaning than in the current context. When Hosea
said, "When Israel was a child, then I loved him, and called
my son out of Egypt" (11:1), he was referring to the Exodus.
This was the context in which the people understood him.
Later, Matthew quoted Hosea's words when he recorded

Jesus' flight from Herod and subsequent return. The words of Hosea applied with equal truth to this later situation. This event in the life of Jesus was a fulfilment of them. In the Syro-Ephraimitic crisis Isaiah promised Ahaz that a child should be born that would be a sign to the people. What Isaiah meant cannot be certain, but his promise of Immanuel was certainly fulfilled in Jesus of Nazareth. The people who heard the description of the Suffering Servant in Isaiah 53 could not comprehend the prophetic depth of the words. The "servant" may have been a contemporary political or religious leader. The promise was completely realized in Jesus Christ, Redeemer, Saviour, and Lord.

Those who heard Haggai may have construed his words as a promise of earthly riches. But the true fulfilment of the prophet's words was found in the personal Messiah, the Prince of peace. It is significant that as Haggai continued describing the future glory of the second Temple, he said, "In this place will I give peace, saith the Lord of hosts" (v. 9).

The early scholars who recognized a messianic strain in such passages as these cannot be discounted or minimized. And the "first hearers" understood even less because the veil was still over their eyes. Men in this day can sing without any sense of incongruity Wesley's great words:

> Come, Desire of nations, come!
> Fix in us Thy humble home:
> Rise, the woman's conquering seed,
> Bruise in us the serpent's head.

Clyde Franciso beautifully and ably contends, that "the Old Testament mysteriously says that God is both one and plural" and "later revelation in Christ pictures God as one and three." Is it not just as true that spiritual insight in interpreting reveals that Haggai was actually promising more than the wealth of the heathen nations? He was telling the discouraged builders of the coming of a personal Messiah to adorn their Temple.

Evaluation (2:10–19)

This third discourse of Haggai contains a striking parable from Levitical law. The application is unique. If one bears holy flesh in the skirt of his garment and touches food with the skirt, it will not make the food holy. If, however, one who is unclean because he has touched a dead body shall touch this food, it will become unclean. The prophet is saying that infection is more contagious than cure.

What relevance did this parable have for the people of Judah? In all probability, Haggai's emphasis and concern were not merely for the rules of the Levitical law on external purity and the fulfilment of ritual acts. His concept of morality was deeper than the legalistic code. Nor was he likely to be referring to the Samaritans and their desire to offer assistance in building the Temple. Hardly could he have been inferring that the people were still in rebellion to the Lord or that some of the group had defiled themselves and thus had spread defilement to the entire company of builders. The interpretation is far more practical and related to the attitude of the people. Haggai was illustrating a deep principle.

The Jews had been negligent in building God's house. The prophet had reminded them of the chastisements that had come and related them to the people's woeful neglect of duty. The people repented, began the work, and then expected immediate prosperity in material things. When it did not come, they became discouraged and began to complain. Haggai declared that life is not that simple. Automatic and immediate affluence is not the result of turning to God and seeking his will. This principle is true for both individuals and nations. Raymond Calkins says, "One may turn from his wickedness and seek to do the will of God and yet continue to suffer because of a sinful past. The infectious power of evil may persist even after one has undertaken to live a holy life."

S. L. Edgar sees in this passage a truth which he calls a most important religious principle. Indirect contact with holiness is not sufficient to make one holy. One's parents may have been dedicated Christians, possessing a personal and intimate relationship with Christ, but this does not guarantee that the children will have an equally vital Christian faith. One may feel the impact of a parent's faith and be influenced by it, but each must experience new birth and personal faith in Christ. The New Testament teaches nothing of proxy faith. Edgar says, "It is not a property of Christian faith that once it is found in a family it is secure for generations. Each succeeding generation must itself come to terms with God." Although this was not the paramount truth emphasized by Haggai, it is a legitimate observation and a worthwhile lesson to be gleaned from this section.

In summary, Haggai was earnestly urging the people to reevaluate their conduct as a nation, to consider God's dealings with them and to look forward to greater blessings in deeper dedication to God's purposes for them. They must not expect too much too soon. The road ahead was long and difficult, but the assuring fact of God's presence would lighten the load and make the rough places smooth.

Exaltation (2:20–23)

Haggai's final message for his people was delivered on the same day as the preceding one. The concluding word is to Zerubbabel the governor. He was the grandson of king Jehoiachin, and thus was in the direct line of David's descendants. Since he was the governor of Judah he was, therefore, the civil ruler. Many competent scholars believe he is the Shesh-bazzar who was appointed by Cyrus, but other equally competent ones think he was his successor.

The last oracle of Haggai was a promise to Zerubbabel that he would receive personal honor and exaltation. The passage is messianic in tone and content. Haggai returned to the theme of the second oracle. There would be a shaking of the heavens and the earth. The throne of the heathen kingdoms would be overthrown. When this takes place, Zerubbabel would be exalted and given a place of distinction. The Lord had chosen him and would make him a signet—the most highly cherished of all possessions to an Oriental. He guarded it constantly, wearing it on his finger or attaching it to a cord fastened around his neck and letting it hang near his heart. This promise meant that Zerubbabel had been chosen by God for special favor. He would keep him under his protecting care. The solemnity of this truth and the assurance of its fulfilment was indicated by the threefold repetition of the phrase "saith the Lord" in the last verse. This is surely God's word!

The purpose of such a promise was to reaffim the messianic hope and identify the House of David with this hope. God was still alive and had not forgotten nor forsaken his people. Every generation needs to be reminded afresh of this truth.

For Further Reading
♣

CALKINS, RAYMOND. *The Modern Message of the Minor Prophets*. New York: Harper & Bros., 1947.

DAVIDSON, A. B. *The Books of Nahum, Habakkuk and Zephaniah*. Cambridge: University Press, 1920.

EISELEN, FREDERICK. *Commentary on the Old Testament, Vol. IX*. New York: Eaton and Mains, 1907.

HASTINGS, JAMES. *The Speaker's Bible*. Aberdeen: "The Speaker's Bible" Office, 1930.

JEFFERSON, CHARLES. *The Minister as Prophet*. New York: Grosset & Dunlap, 1933.

KENNEDY, JAMES H. *Studies in the Book of Jonah*. Nashville: Broadman Press, 1956.

LAETSCH, THEODORE. *Bible Commentary, the Minor Prophets*. St. Louis: Concordia Publishing House, 1956.

PATERSON, JOHN. *The Goodly Fellowship of the Prophets*. New York: Scribner's, 1948.

PUSEY, E. B. *The Minor Prophets*. Grand Rapids: Baker Book House, 1953.

SKINNER, JOHN. *Prophecy & Religion*. Cambridge: University Press, 1948.

SMITH, ROY L. *The Future Is Upon Us*. Nashville: Abingdon, 1962.

STEWART, JAMES S. *The Strong Name*. New York: Charles Scribner's Sons, 1941.

TRUEBLOOD, ELTON. *The Life We Prize*. New York: Harper & Bros., 1951.

VAN ZELLER, DOM HUBERT. *The Outspoken Ones*. New York: Sheed & Ward, 1955.

WOLFE, ROLLAND E. *Meet Amos and Hosea*. New York: Harper & Bros., 1945.

WOLFENDALE, JAMES. *A Homilectic Commentary on the Minor Prophets*. New York: Funk & Wagnalls. (n.d.)

YATES, KYLE M. *Preaching from the Prophets*. Nashville: Broadman Press, 1942.